"THE HIGHER CHRISTIAN LIFE"

SOURCES FOR THE STUDY OF THE HOLINESS, PENTECOSTAL, AND KESWICK MOVEMENTS

*A forty-eight-volume facsimile
series reprinting extremely
rare documents for the study of
nineteenth-century religious
and social history, the rise
of feminism, and the
history of the Pentecostal and
Charismatic movements*

Edited by

Donald W. Dayton
Northern Baptist Theological Seminary

Advisory Editors

D. William Faupel, *Asbury Theological Seminary*
Cecil M. Robeck, Jr., *Fuller Theological Seminary*
Gerald T. Sheppard, *Union Theological Seminary*

A GARLAND SERIES

THE LAST
GREAT CONFLICT

A. J. Tomlinson

Garland Publishing, Inc.
New York & London
1985

For a complete list of the titles in this series
see the final pages of this volume.

This facsimile has been made from a copy at
the Church of God of Prophesy, Cleveland, Tenn.

Library of Congress Cataloging in Publication Data

Tomlinson, A. J.
THE LAST GREAT CONFLICT.

("The Higher Christian life")
Reprint. Originally published: Cleveland, Tenn. :
Press of W.E. Rodgers, 1913.
1. Church of God—Doctrines.   2. Church of God—History.
3. Church of God (Cleveland, Tenn.)—Doctrines.
4. Church of God (Cleveland, Tenn.)—History.
I. Title.   II. Series.
BX7034.T65   1985   289.9   85-4497
ISBN 0-8240-6446-1 (alk. paper)

The volumes in this series are printed on
acid-free, 250-year-life paper.

Printed in the United States of America

A. J. Tomlinson

THE

LAST GREAT CONFLICT.

BY

A. J. TOMLINSON,

Editor of "The Church of God Evangel."

"And I saw heaven opened, and behold a white horse; and he that sat upon him was called Faithful and True, and in righteousness he did judge and make war. * * * * * * * * * And the armies which were in heaven followed him upon white horses, clothed in fine linen, white and clean. And out of his mouth goeth a sharp sword, that with it he should smite the nations: and he shall rule them."—Rev. 19:11, 14, 15.

CLEVELAND, TENN.
PRESS OF WALTER E. RODGERS.
1913.

DEDICATION.

TO the Church of God, whose duty it is to preach the gospel of the kingdom in all the world for a witness, and then be presented to Jesus Christ, "A glorious church, not having spot, or wrinkle, or any such thing,"

THIS VOLUME IS HUMBLY DEDICATED
BY ITS AUTHOR.

CONTENTS.

PREFACE.

Forasmuch as many others have taken in hand to set forth things which are believed by them, it seemed good to me also, to write these pages, both to those who need instruction and those who need stimulation and inspiration.

It is our purpose to encourage both men and women, young and old; to undertake great things for God and expect great things from God. If these pages are the means of causing one person to venture out, and to aspire to greater usefulness in the service of God and the evangelization of this world, we will not think them written in vain.

We do not send forth this volume as a literary production, neither do we claim for it perfection in language, but we have meant to convey our thoughts in simple language, so it could be easily understood.

While writing, after much prayer and weeping before God, we have hoped that underneath every word would be a hidden power that would have a tendency to attract the readers more than the words themselves. We hope the same Spirit that inspired the writer will so envelope the reader that they two may be made one, and that a real knitting together may be the result for the glory of God, in answer to the prayer of our Lord.

It is with a heart full of love that we greet you,

whether friend or foe. No matter how much you may differ in your views, we trust that every one will be so freighted with love, that, by the time you are through, you will feel yourself so thrilled with the Spirit of our Master, that both reader and writer will be melted into one.

It is not too much to expect this to have a place amid the multitude of religious volumes. We do not expect it to take the place of any that has gone before, but only to fill its little mission among the millions of others.

We have not meant to imitate, neither is it intended just to fill up space, nor was it written because of having idle time to spend; but rather because of an unseen impelling power that pressed it upon us amid the hurry and rush of other duties, until much has been done at late hours of the night while the millions of earth were taking their rest.

May He who is able to make "weak things" "confound the mighty," and the "things that are not" "bring to naught the things that are," breathe, by His Spirit, upon these chapters, and fan them into a flame of fire for His glory.

THE AUTHOR.

The Last Great Conflict.

CHAPTER I.

OPENING CHAPTER.

Satan is mustering his forces and drafting every man and woman into his service that is possible for him to procure. The smoke of an awful battle is already rising from the battle field where the skirmishers are engaged. But it is now high time for the regulars, to advance with the full equipment of Pentecost, and to pour into the ranks of the enemy the shot and shell, grape and canister of gospel truth and power until the roar of the cannons can be heard all over the world as they belch forth with tremendous fury their deadly discharges.

Now while so many are deserting for the want of true godly, and may I say, manly courage, when the battle has barely begun, is the time for the true and noble soldiers to take a bolder stand.

Soldiers of a country enlist in the army to obey their commander, get shot and die.

Our Commander is cheering us on and still sounding out the thrilling, soulstirring command to "Go ye * * teach all nations * * Teaching them to observe all things whatsoever I have commanded you."

No matter about the fury of the enemy, nor the scary boldness he presents to estrange the weaker ones from their purpose, or the tremendous onslaught he is waging against full Pentecostal teachings, the command still rings out from our all conquering Captain and King—"Go ye!"

'Press the battle' as a slogan or war-cry should be taken up by every lover of truth and echoed and re-echoed over every plain and hilltop until those who have had a tendency to compromise healing, tongues, the gifts of the Spirit etc. will become ashamed, ask forgiveness of their Captain, raise the red flag of war and rush into the battle with a holy zeal such as no people of past history have ever manifested.

We must stand bravely for divine healing according to the Scriptures. Many have weakened because of a failure sometimes to see immediate results. The doctrine of "healing" is true if we all die. We had better obey God and die than disobey Him and live. "And others were tortured, not accepting deliverance; that they might obtain a better resurrection." (Heb. 11:35).

It is one thing to hear of the truth of healing in the atonement and know about it, and rejoice in it while in good health, and another thing to be delivered into the hands of Satan, as was dear old brother Job, and stand true in the test. "And the Lord said unto Satan, Behold, he is in thine hand." (Job 2:6.) Three worlds are to be convinced that we will stand true in the severest test and the last great conflict with the enemy. The way this test is made is for the devil to settle down upon our bodies in sickness, placing his cruel fangs upon our vitals; and when we pray, or call for the elders of the church and they pray, anoint with oil and lay their hands on according to the Scripture, and we have done perfectly what the Bible says, still obtain no relief from the awful suffering. That was evidently Job's condition. Although at that time the prescriptions that we now have in Mark and James were not given, but true men of God resorted to Him for healing just the same and used no other remedy.

God had acknowledged Job to be "Perfect and upright, fearing God and eschewing evil." This fact is recorded in not less than three places in the book of Job. Then he was not sick and covered "with sore boils from the sole of his feet unto his crown" because of his disobedience to God, but rather to prove to the devil and millions of inhabitants of the three worlds that a man would stand true to God under a severe and extreme test. Job's experience is left on record for our benefit.

I was called home from the Bahama Islands, where I was engaged in giving those precious people the gospel of Jesus, on account of the severe illness of my wife. She had suffered for twenty-four hours constantly the agonies of death over and over again, and in this awful trial and test, with husband away, she refused every remedy but the Bible way. Eight times she had similar attacks, lasting from eight to twenty-four hours. The worst finally came. For about ten hours we wrestled and fought against demon powers which caused the awful suffering and most excruciating pain. Having taken no medicine that would have a tendency to stupify her she was at her right mind all the time, but for hours she was like a raving maniac on account of the severest suffering and pain. She endured the agony, obeyed the Word, stood the test, until our Refiner, who was standing by, saw it was enough and bade the arch-enemy release his grasp and depart. Oh what a calm! A peaceful, blessed, welcome calm! "Made perfect through suffering" comes to my mind so forcibly, that I must write it here. She lay quiet for an hour as if she would soon pass away to be with Jesus. Then with feeble voice whispered her desire to have all the church and her friends to come to her bedside as she had "a message and a blessing for everyone." As they came, the Spirit came upon her and for five hours she took one after another by the hand and delivered to them the message and blessing.

She had endured the suffering and was. left so weak she could scarcely speak above a whisper, but

that my redeemer liveth, and that he shall stand at the latter day upon the earth: and though after my skin worms destroy this body, yet in my flesh shall I see God." (Job 19:25,26.)

Teach divine healing? Yes! Practice it and no other, live or die? Yes! Yes!! Amen!!! Be bolder in it than ever! This is fighting the enemy on his own territory, bearding the lion in his den, in the last great conflict. "It is appointed unto man once to die," then bravely die for the truth, as men by the thousands have died for their country, marching right up to the roaring cannons as they belched forth their deadly carnage, merely because they have sworn to obey their captain.

Dear friend, haven't you sworn to obey the commands of your Lord? Doesn't He tell you what to do in case of sickness? And does He say if that fails to call for a physician? Answer for yourself. You surely know the Bible on this point. If you do not, then you are a very poor soldier. In the army, and the battle likely to overtake you any moment, and you don't know the tactics of war? You had better learn them quickly. He would make a poor soldier who enlisted in the army and would not learn the tactics of war.

Poor christian! that has enlisted in His service and will not accept, learn and practice divine healing, but will resort to other means, and just as really disobey God as Adam and Eve did in the garden of of Eden.

Remember we are now in the last great conflict. Now is the time to press the battle and wage a strong warfare against the devil and all his allurements and devices. Die rather than go contrary to the plain teaching in God's Word! If you should die for the truth it would be no more than thousands have done before you. Then you would obtain a better resurrection. (Heb. 11:35.)

Intrepid faith and undaunted courage are the great needs of these stupendous days that are now upon us. The devil is against us. The world is against us, and the popular christian religion is against us; but we are in the conflict and must fight or die and fight if we do die. "The last enemy is death." (1 Cor. 15:26.) We must conquer him. The battle is to be fought for and in the name of Jesus. If we should fall in the struggle, lose our lives for the sake of being obedient to our Captain in this awful conflict, we shall save them. "But whosoever will lose his life for my sake, the same shall save it." (Luke 9:24.)

Live by the Bible or die by the Bible, yea, whether we live or die, if we obey Him we are true soldiers of Jesus Christ: and we are His for service because we have enlisted in His army. "For whether we live, we live unto the Lord; and whether we die, we die unto the Lord: whether we live therefore, or die, we are the Lord's." (Rom. 14:8.)

Another source of the enemy's onslaught against us is the "tongues" as evidence of the baptism with the Holy Ghost. We must courageously press the battle on that point, and become bolder and bolder in teaching this truth, for there is a great temptation and tendency to compromise, or at least quiet down on that particular point.

The religious press is against us. The world's press is against us. The ministers of all denominations, of a hundred millions strong, are in opposition to this truth. The independent holiness press and ministry are all against us, but the conflict is on, and we dare not retreat and forsake our Captain, and leave Him to fight on the field alone. The red flag of truth and uncompromising boldness and undaunted courage and holy zeal must float over every nation and clime, declaring emphatically that no one ever has or ever will receive the baptism with the Holy Ghost without the speaking in other tongues accompanying as the evidence.

Let the enemy raise his war whoop and turn his gatling guns of false teaching and a hireling ministry against us, we must and will march right up to the ramparts and over the breastworks, snatch the sword (Word of God) out of the giant's hands, and with it cut off his head. Glory! In God is our strength.   We do not fear men nor devils with God at our side and Jesus, "the Lion of the tribe of Judah," as our "King Emmanuel."

He, whose name is "Wonderful, Counsellor, The mighty God, The everlasting Father, The Prince of Peace;" He, who rides the "white horse" down from the skies with the "sharp sword in His mouth" as He orders the battle; He, who is the all conquering King and Lord of Lords, tells us to "Go ye therefore, and teach all nations, baptizing them in the name of the Father, and of the Son, and of the Holy Ghost: Teaching them to observe ALL things whatsoever I have commanded you: and lo, I am with you alway, even unto the end of the world. Amen."   (Math. 28:19, 20.)

CHAPTER II.

ABOUNDING LOVE.

There is much spoken and written in these days on the subject of divine love. With all that has been spoken and written on this subject the depth of this wonderful attribute of God has never been explored by man. With all that has ever been experienced by the noble saints who have lived and died and gone to glory, there is still a supply and depth of this peculiar gem that lies unused and untouched.

In Joseph, with his display of love for his older brothers, in supplying them with food after they had treated him so cruelly, is only a very faint display of this grand and glorious virtue.

The sweet singer of Israel who ran from his assailant, and sang and made music for his enemy rather than show any signs of revolt or vengeance; he who could have risen up against Saul and taken his life and thus made his accession to the throne sure and hastened it on; this David, who was loved and revered by the thousands of Israel and the inhabitants of other nations as well, who commanded the respect of all who lived in his day and every generation since; and who is loved and respected and almost worshipped by multitudes today, was possessed with only a small amount of divine love in comparison to the abundance stored away, and really placed at the disposal of all people of every age.

John the beloved disciple, whom Jesus loved. and who has used the word "love" in his writings more than any other writer of the sacred pages of the Holy Bible, perhaps plunged deeper into this wonderful experience than any other one who has ever lived, and yet in his writings, just under the surface, can be detected some indications that he himself felt a shortness in the possession of this wonderful experience. And although he was so saturated with it, both soul and body, that boiling oil would have no effect upon him when, to destroy him, his persecutors threw him into a caldron of boiling oil with a hope of ridding themselves and their generation of such a man of love and God; yet in him was probably not the deepest form of divine love.

After all that has been written on this wonderful theme, by men who were inspired by the Holy Ghost, as well as men of high abilities and attainments, I am surprised at myself as I reflect and really find that I am writing a few words on the greatest subject that has ever been presented to man.

With my feeling of inability and shortness of experience I can only traverse the surface, but one thing that gives me encouragement to continue is that I can be as an index finger pointing onward and inward, showing to those who come in contact with me that my vision of faith beholds greater, grander and more glorious possessions a little farther on, and perhaps some one may be induced to make a greater sacrifice, and plunge deeper into the debris and obstructions that prevent the obtaining of the "pearl of great price," than they otherwise would if I had never spoken or written on the subject.

I have only occasional glimpses of the beautiful estate of which I write, but they are enough to urge me on with a hope that, if not before, at least the final plunge through the "twinkling of an eye" change, or death, will put me into this wonderful realm of love and glory of which I write.

God is love, and in proportion to our possession of Him and His presence here in this world is this love realized and displayed. "God so loved the world that He gave His only begotten Son," and "in Him dwelleth all the fullness of the Godhead bodily."

God gave His Son to and for this world; then love gave love. God has then given love in its fullness to us, and in and through Christ it is attainable, and can be realized and possessed by those who have obtained all the fullness of God.

The display of love that was in Jesus was so extreme that the human mind has not been, and never will be able to grasp it in its fullest sense; yet as this great treasure has been displayed in full measure in Jesus Christ, by His divine power and unreasonable methods it has been, and is placed by Him, within the reach of him who is willing to go through all the changes and departments of suffering that is required to gain such possession.

An example of its sacrifice is seen in its fullness only in Jesus. While we have good examples in the lives, works and sacrifices of the apostles and thousands of others besides, who have given their possessions in this world as well as their lives, yet the fullness is only manifested in the blessed Son of God. He left His rich possessions in glory and plunged Himself to the opposite extreme, becoming the "poorest of men." He left position and honor and came down to the most lowly servitude, and upon Him was heaped dishonor and disgrace, and He "learned * * * obedience by the things which he suffered." This is a very peculiar statement, and by us incomprehensible. Having had all knowledge; having had all abilities; having known obedience to the very extreme limit, even beyond that of Abraham, who, in obedience to God's voice, took his own son Isaac and offered him as a sacrifice on Mt. Moriah, and yet He, the Christ of God, learned obedience. Truly, without controversy, great is the mystery of Godliness."

His indefatigable efforts to relieve suffering humanity, by healing their diseases, casting devils out of them, feeding the multitudes who were hungry, and finally as a climax gave His life on the cruel and rugged cross to obtain eternal redemption for us, is truly an example worthy of notice.

He went to the very lowest disgrace in the eyes of men, that of being crucified. Not only did He descend to the very lowest position of disgrace and dishonor in the sight of men, but there is evidence given by words that fell from His sacred lips during His last moments on the cross as He said, "Eli, Eli, lama sabach-thani? that is to say, My God, my God, why hast thou forsaken me?" that He went to the very lowest dishonor and disgrace in the sight of God; so low, so degraded, to such a low disgraced estate, that even God refused to look upon Him.

Such a display of love on the part of our Savior is beyond the comprehension of our finite minds; but we are to go beyond our understanding and comprehension, if we go into the mystery of godliness and pass into "the love of Christ which passeth knowledge." It evidently takes this extreme experience in the realm of divine love to place us in the experience for which our hearts are crying out and our prayers are ascending; that state of being "filled with all the fullness of God." Not until our lives are saturated with divine love are we even approaching anyways near the desired haven.

While we are always and forever in favor of the physical operations by the Spirit; the speaking in tongues as the evidence of the baptism with the Holy Ghost, the casting out of devils, healing the sick by the laying on of hands, etc., yet there is a realm beyond that embodies all. While "without faith it is impossible to please God, and without hope all humanity would grope about in sad despair, yet beyond all, in the valley of humility, unexplored and unpossessed, is a silent force, a glorious virtue, a rich possession, a "pearl of great price," that human language can ne'er describe and human minds can never comprehend. This possession, this silent but all powerful force, this "pearl of great price" is Divine Love. "And now abideth faith, hope, love, these three; but the greatest of these is love."

There is something here in this realm that we are approaching as we write that reminds one of the half hour of silence in heaven. "Tread softly, you are on holy ground," seems to ring sweetly and specially pleasant in our inner ear. A feeling of breathless stillness is creeping over my entire being; a power within seems to be surging, filling my throat with a lump, eyes with tears and pen with inspiration as I write on this greatest of all themes. The wonder is now that I ever attempted such an arduous task. God alone inspires; God alone shall have the glory.

We would not underestimate the value of other themes and minor experiences and manifestations of God's presence, power and glory; but one thing is certain, we cannot overestimate the value of divine love. We have ventured back in behind the veil and we are lothe to return. Although the words written fail to express—although the theme is almost dishonored by our using it, yet there is a depth in it that can never be expressed, but thank God it is attainable and can be realized.

I'm sure a revival of love is needful everywhere. Such a deep sense of love, such a saturation of love that would silence the tongue in times of the deepest distress and trial; that would forever put an end to fault finding, mote hunting, backbiting, chafing, ungodly conversation, hypocracy and false teaching.

We have the Bible; many of us know its teachings on primary lines. We have heard preaching on almost all lines of truth. We have seen the manifestations of the Spirit. All these are essential and have their respective places; but all have failed to bring unity, power, and the fulness of Pentecost, so our hearts are still crying out for the "pearl of great price," to "be filled with all the fulness of God."

A sufficiency of this love will make any sacrifice for God and his glory seem but a mere speck. Our lives will be given entirely for His service. No jesting, no joking, no light chaffy conversation, no melancholy, no complaints, no murmuring or grumbling, no disorder, no display of self and no desire for selfish worldly pleasures; but our affections will really be placed upon things above.

That which never fails should be earnestly sought for and obtained. We should not be idle about this matter. Souls, that might be won for God and heaven, are plunging into eternal destruction because we are so slow in the purchase of this that never fails. This world is dying and going to hell for want of love. They must be loved. They must know they are loved. While christian? people are divided and caviling over minor differences satan is busy carrying off the multitudes into eternal punishment. Can we afford it? Can't we stop it? The great problem of our day is solved and victory perched upon our banners as they float in the breeze, as we wave them around the one word and experience LOVE!

> There is a way that leads to life,
>   There is a way to find it;
> Abounding love is always rife,
>   And always will provide it.

CHAPTER III.

THE WORLD IS LOST.

We do not write the above title because we think our readers are ignorant of the fact, but rather to remind them of that theme which they already know, and if possible to stimulate them to the putting forth of more energy and the making of more sacrifices to spread this glorious gospel in obedience to the command of our Lord and King.

We acknowledge that the masses of the people are in total ignorance of the Christ of the Bible, and that there is only one way by which they may be found and saved. Then to be loyal subjects of the King the inhabitants of the Kingdom must obey the voice or commands of their King.

When we really begin to recount the people of the world by sections, nations and continents, we get a view of the reality of the vast millions much better than to merely glance at the world as a whole. Think of the multitudes of towns in the United States alone, with from five to ten thousand inhabitants, to say nothing about the larger cities of from forty to five hundred thousand; and Chicago and New York with their millions, besides the rural districts, many of which are also thickly settled that conversation can be carried on by the neighbors as they stand in the doors of their houses.

The United States with nearly one hundred million population is only like a "drop in the bucket"
in comparison with the whole world. The human
mind is not able to grasp the great sea of humanity
that is thronging this globe to-day. Think of China
with her teeming millions, where it is said there are
nine hundred walled cities without the gospel; and
Africa, a great continent swarming with inhabitants
that no doubt has many, many inland tribes that have
scarcely been discovered by the civilized world.
South America, "the neglected continent," is a
dwelling place for multitudes that are so hidden by
the luxurient growth of forests and other barriers
that a trace of them has never been recorded, except by signs pointing inward showing that there
are still more beyond. Only recently a village of
two-thousand inhabitants was discovered by a rub-
ber tradesman after days of travel beyond what
seemed to be the borders of the existance of human
life. There are also the islands of the sea besides
all the great continants with their teeming millions.

As I sit on the shore of the Biscayne bay and look
out on the broad expanse of the Atlantic ocean and
think of the countries the shores of which are
washed by her waves; and still go beyond and
trace the shores of the broad Pacific, also the Indian
ocean, and remember the countries that lie around

them with all their inhabitants that are to be saved only by Jesus Christ or spend eternity in hell with the damned my heart almost fails me. Oh, the waste of human life! Oh, the lost opportunities! One soul passing into eternal torments at every pulsation of the heart. To me the awfulness of it is enexpressible.

There are thousands and probably millions who have heard of the tender, gentle Savior and have accepted Him, but there are millions more who must hear and have a chance to accept or reject Him for this Gospel of the Kingdom must be taken into all the world. It is true the task is great, but it must be done. It is not too much to say it must be done in our day. This task has been shifted from one generation to another long enough. It is up to us now. Our commander says "Go!" The sacrifices must be made. Ease, pleasures, friends we love, homes and all their comforts must be forsaken by those whom God calls.

Money that has been hoarded up must be put into use. This is the time for the last message to go forth and it must go. Some who cannot go must send. It is no time to leave legacies and estates for children yet unborn. Everything must be put into the one great effort to take the gospel to all the world. This should be the theme and object of every christian. To be or act contrary to this will only prove disloyalty to the Christ who said, "This gospel shall be preached in all the world." To fail to put forth every effort and bend all of our energies in that direction means to fail Him who gave the command. Oh, if the christian people could only realize their responsibility; if they could only realize the worth of one human soul, there would be a rattling of coins and passing of checks as has never been known in the business world!

We are not half awake. While some have sacrificed homes and kindred, and others have given a few dollars for their support, yet with all this, I feel safe in saying that the very best of us, the most zealous, even, are not half awake. Take into consideration the great missionary movements that are now on among the churches, and the enthusiastic, untiring efforts made by those who are volunteering to go and are going with no promise for support from churches or missionary boards, stimulated by the experience received since the falling of the "latter rain," and still I can say without the fear of successful contradiction, we are not half awake.

When we fully realize the value of souls, the awfulness of hell, and have attained such a love for Jesus that His words will sink into our hearts like stones into water, then and not until then will we really awake to the full responsibility that is now resting heavy upon us. We are so slow! Millions are dropping into hell that could have been rescued while we are studying and planning what to do.

If the firemen in our cities were as slow to act in their sphere as we are in ours, they would be "fired" at once and a new crew selected. In every department of the business world it is hurry, hurry for the sake of money making or pleasure; but when it comes to carrying this gospel of the kingdom in all the world it is anything else but hurry. Those who would hurry about giving, and sometimes do give all they have, are perplexed because they have nothing to give.

My soul is all aflame, to some degree at least, with His love for this lost world as I write at this midnight hour after spending the day in His service. Sleep has gone from me. Souls are dropping into hell at the rate of 3,600 every hour—86,400 every day, how can any one sleep? Jesus spent whole nights in prayer over this lost world. Tears of sorrow were shed by Him over the little city of Jerusalem because they would not hear and heed the gospel message. But there are multitudes to-day that would gladly hear it if we could only get to them. Many are weeping now because they can't go. Some who have consecrated their lives to His service are waiting for the means and weeping over a lost world while they wait. Others, whose hearts are in the work, and are willing to go, are unable

to go because of a lack of qualification, prepara-
tion and ability.

But the work must be done. We must get it into
our hearts. It is not a time now to shift the responsibility on to another future generation. We must
do it now in our own generation. We can do it if
we will. When all of God's people really get the fullness of what the one hundred and twenty, the three
thousand and the five thousand and the multitudes both of men and women had, they will go
everywhere and preach this gospel of the kingdom
as a witness. The great wave of Pentecostal power
and glory is coming. There is a lull and a calm
just now; we are going up grade, but listen: "There
is a sound of abundance of rain." The little cloud
has been seen. Gird up thy loins and run before
the chariots and carry the good news.

We hear of wrecks, divisions and disgraces among
those who have been recognized as Pentecostal
people, but never mind that, God does not wreck,
neither is He divided. He will get a crowd of
faithful followers for this last great conflict that will
neither wreck, divide nor disgrace. Thank God!
Hallelujah! We are now in the time of the culmi-
nation of events. The time of the consummation.
Some may fail and suffer defeat but not all will fail.
Some made a shipwreck of faith in the days of Paul,
but a sufficient number stood true, in the midst of

awful tests and persecutions to carry the same gospel we now have to every creature under heaven. (Col. 1:23.) They did it then, and when God's people get the same identical experience enjoyed by the early disciples, they will do it again.

"Deeper yet," should ring in every soul that has the least bit of love for Jesus. Not only for our own benefit but by going deeper in divine things more souls will be reached and this glorious gospel extended to every nation on earth. Have you enlisted in the fight? Then never shrink or give it up. Fight until you win or die on the field! We are not, and never will be as successful as we should be if we do not get this message into all the world in our day. You are looking for Jesus to come, then assist in some way to spread the news, for the longer we are in getting this great work accomplished the more He will be delayed in closing up this age.

Come on friends, let us put our whole souls and all our abilities into this one thing and make one tremendous effort and accomplish this arduous task and have it over so we will be ready for something else. This one task will be upon us until it is conquered; then let us put forth all our energy and meet conditions that will give us power for the conflict and get it off our hands. With a threshing machine in perfect operation; with its cylinder, windmill, screens, etc., each part performing its function or duty and the sheaves of wheat thrust into its mouth by the feeder, the beautiful grain will appear in its proper place ready for the garner. So when the Church gets in perfect order as it was in apostolic days, the gospel will go forth and souls by the multitudes will be gathered in. Then let us earnestly contend for the faith once delivered to the saints and never rest on our oars, nor stack our arms until we can say, and it can be recorded as a fact: "This gospel of the kingdom has been preached in all the world for a witness, through mighty signs and wonders, by the power of the spirit of God, (Rom. 15:19), and the work Jesus gave us to do has really been accomplished."

CHAPTER IV.

LATENT POWERS.

Within the breasts of the people of this generation dormantly lies possibilities, which if not discovered, brought forth and utilized will rob man-
kind of much good.

Men of science teach and believe that there are
great stores of treasures hidden in the earth and sea
and sky, for the use of man, undiscovered and un-
developed, and are proving their belief in this by
making continuous research. Holes are being
drilled in the earth beneath; soundings and search
by means of divers and glasses are in constant use
in seeking for the discovery of the unknown in the
sea.

Men are not only looking at the material within
their reach on the surface of the earth and below
the surface, but they also have a distinguished upward gaze. We are told that powerful guns have
been dragged up the mountain sides to the highest
peaks and placed with the muzzel upward, heavy
charges poured into them, which, when discharged
hurled the balls with such velocity that they pierced
holes in the sky to an unknown height. Plans have
been formulated for attaching wires to these balls
with a hope of forming a channel or medium by

which something of the unknown could travel like a flash of lightning down to the home of man while the ball was at its greatest height.

For years balloons have been harnessed and loaded with human life, cleaving the sky to a great height, the inmates risking their lives in a little basket hung to a mere canvass loaded with hot air or gas; all with a hope of discovering that which is out of reach of the ordinary walks and attainments of life. In recent years the airships or flying machines are making their way through the upper regions carrying their load of precious freight in the form of human flesh, the intellect of which have ambitions pent up within their own knowledge, with a hope of discovering something of the unknown to harness it for the use and development of man.

As Columbus ventured out from pleasant surroundings into the high seas in search of a shorter passage to the rich spices of India, and instead brought to the knowledge of the inhabitants of the eastern hemisphere the rich country in which we dwell, which has proven to be the best and grandest country of the world, so men are looking downward, and upward. They are bounding and plowing through the unknown above with aspirations no doubt in many cases that are never whispered to the dearest friends lest they should be mocked or met with attempts to discourage.

Astronomers are not idle in their sphere of discovery, but are constantly producing new and more powerful glasses for the purpose of discovering, if possible, new worlds with their inhabitants and peculiar genius that even if there may be no way of communication, their systems, plans or customs might be discovered and brought down to our world for use.

Wireless telegraphy is another factor in the hands of man by which it is hoped that they may be able to so attune their instuments that they will harmonize with and cause to vibrate the cords of a similar instrument operated by the inhabitants of Mars or some of the other planets.

In the physical world men are spending sleepless nights and hazarding their lives with a hope of making some valuable discovery. Men of inventive genius have shut themselves up with no food or companions, while they engaged their mind on some scheme while the train of thought was available, lest a disturbance would cause a disconnection and the whole train of thought be cut asunder and the model in the mind entirely lost before it could become a litteral fact that had form and could be observed.

No disturbance is raised; no umbrage is taken against any of the aforesaid ventures, no matter how insane the views and undertakings, but the world looks on with admiration and applause. Even great

rewards are offered for new and valued inventions.
Thus the physical world is moving on to higher at-
taiments and into a broader sphere of knowledge
every year. Pick and shovel, augur and drill, powder
and dynamite are brought into use to unearth the
unobserved. Diving-bells and torpedo-boats are
assisting men down in the depths of the sea. Balloons and airships are carrying them above in the
air, all in search of the unseen and unknown. The
physical world is full of excitement, wild prophesies
and projects.

Should the spiritual world allow their contem-
poraries to out-wit them? Should the christian
world fold their hands in slumber, sleep long and
eat plentifully, and allow the world by going hungry
and arising early, to win the prize for energy, wit,
longsuffering, perseverance, grit and determination?
Jesus said, "The children of this world are, in their
generation wiser than the children of light." But
should it be so? With the same untiring effort on
the part of the christian world, many of the unseen
and unknown blessings in God's eternal store-house
might be discovered and harnessed for the glory of
God, the use of man and for the hastening of the
return of our Lord. Latent powers are now lying
dormant, unused and unknown in the bosoms and
within the reach of many, many today.

Within the grain of wheat is a germ of life, fraught

with great possibilities for the sustenance of man by a continual growth and increase as it is placed in the soil, where that germ of life will burst forth into real action. I just feel so with many young lives of to-day. With proper environments and under certain conditions, those latent powers will spring into use, and not only surprise friends and acquaintances, but will in many instances surprise even the persons themselves, because of the successes and exploits wrought.

The grain of wheat, though in it is that germ of life, can lie dormant in the dry granary, and finally wither, dry up and blow away as dust. So with men and women in the Christian world to-day. Men and women love their homes, their friends and companions; and it is almost impossible to get them out of the old family customs and ruts. Like the grain of wheat, although the possibilities and powers for great achievements and exploits for God are in their breasts, yet they can stay at home and follow in the common rote of life, and finally wither away spiritually, dry up and blow away.

Peter and John ran to the sepulchre, when they heard that Jesus had disappeared, stooped down and entered in and saw the linen clothes and napkin, but afterward quietly came out and walked away to their own homes, and Mary alone tarried until she saw the vision of angels, and a little later the Lord Himself, and held a conversation with Him.

There are gigantic possibilities within our reach in the vast, illimitable and immeasurable realm of grace, if we will only put forth as much energy and effort to explore and search after them as men do in the physical and scientific world. We are accorded the privilege of looking through a more powerful lens than astronomers have ever invented. We can look, if we close our eyes from the seeing of evil, until we can behold the King in His beauty.

The wireless telegraphy and other wonderful and marvelous inventions of man are only mere specks in comparison to that which is attainable by the people of God in this generation. Read the wonderful words of promise: "And to make all men see what is the fellowship (partnership, familiar intercourse) of the mystery, which from the beginning of the world hath been hid in God, who created all things by Jesus Christ: To the intent that now unto principalities and powers in heavenly places might be known BY THE CHURCH the manifold wisdom of God, according to the eternal purpose which he purposed in Christ Jesus our Lord: in whom we have boldness and access with confidence by the faith of him * * * * that ye, being rooted and grounded in love, may be able to comprehend with all saints what is the breadth, and length, and depth, and height; and to know the love of Christ, which passeth knowledge, that ye might be filled with all the fullness of God." (Eph. 3:9-19.)

Farewell scientists. Farewell astronomers. Farewell philosophers. Farewell inventive geniuses, explorers and searchers after the unknown; men of worldly wisdom, wit, ambition and grit. "Now unto him that is able to do exceeding abundantly above all that we ask or think, according to the power (latent or unused; germ of life like is in the grain of wheat) that worketh in us, unto him be glory IN THE CHURCH by Christ Jesus throughout all ages, world without end. Amen." (Eph. 3:20, 21.)

We should certainly aspire to that high position spoken of and described by Paul, that we might attain to that height in the realm of grace that Christ has obtained for us; that He knows we can reach through Him if we bestir ourselves as He knows we can, and that has been placed within our grasp. "Not as though I had already attained (says Paul), either were already perfect: but I follow after, if that I may apprehend that for which also I am apprehended of Christ Jesus." (Phil. 3:12.)

If people would engage themselves in constantly moving on to these higher plains of experience there would be less time for criticism, fault finding, backbiting, caviling over doctrines, and divisions. It is always those who are behind in the race that can see the mistakes, miss-steps and faults of others who are ahead of them. Those who are ahead are so bent on winning the prize that they have no time to look at the faults and mistakes of others, and they are so far ahead in the race that they do not feel the coldness that surrounds the lukewarm and fault finder in the rear.

This world must be evangelized. "This gospel of the kingdom (power) must be preached in all the world," in our day. We must not shift this responsibility to a future generation as all other generations have done. There is enough latent power now in men and women, if brought into use, to evangelize this world in five years and usher in the coming of our King. There are possibilities in our young men and young women, and the middle aged as well, if it were not quenched and locked down by worldly environments, idle matrimony, ungodly and "unequally yoked together" marriages, to fire this world with a fear of God and His power, as Samson's foxes fired the corn fields of the Philistines.

Oh for a million men and women to burst forth, with such holy ambition, with every unused power in full use, like mad-men to strike terror and fear to all the half hearted religionists of the day! John Brown, who with only eighteen men determined to abolish slavery by the seizing of the arsenal at Harper's Ferry, lost his life, but won a place in history because of his boldness and bravery. General Grant rode back and forth on his gallant steed before his great army and cheered and encouraged them on in the battle until the victory was won, although scores and hundreds of his soldiers fell on the field weltering and perishing in their own blood. Should not these daring deeds of reckless bravery put to shame our weak-kneed religious enthusiasm?

Isn't our cause of far greater importance? Shouldn't we be stimulated to the very highest pitch to fight in this most glorious of all battles? Now while we are in the last great conflict can we be satisfied to remain behind where we can see others trudging on in advance, or rushing heedless and reckless into the thickest of the fight? Rouse, ye people! This is the last great conflict! The battle is on! Rush into it to win or die on the field! Look ahead! See the red flag as it waves in the breeze! Behold the enormous possibilities lying unused within your own breast! "PRESS TOWARD THE MARK, FOR THE PRIZE OF THE HIGH CALLING OF GOD IN CHRIST JESUS."

CHAPTER V.

This is not only a subject for discussion, but it is also an experience provided for all, and attainable through Jesus Christ.

While Jesus was "a man of sorrows and acquainted with grief," yet He gives a brief hint that He had joy. He not only spoke of His joy, but expressed a desire for His disciples or followers to be filled with it, and told them how this joy might be obtained. "These things have I spoken unto you, that my joy might remain in you, and that your joy might be full." (Jno. 15:11.) He has given us words or commands which, if we accept and obey them, will give us this experience.

It would be well here to notice the meaning of the word joy. Webster tells us it is "Gladness. Gaiety. The emotion excited from the receiving or expectation of good." Then as people, who have obeyed the words of Jesus, have obtained salvation from sin and have a real experience of grace in their hearts, they have more reason for joy and rejoicing than people of the world.

No doubt the majority of the professing Christians of the world to-day have failed to obtain His joy, because of a failure on their part to get His words and their importance sufficiently implanted on their minds to obey them, therefore, the apparent joy that many show is merely a show, and not an inward natural joy that can be spoken of as His joy.

You will notice that Jesus not only wants His disciples to have His joy remain in them, but wants their joy to be full. Fullness of joy! And yet so many people think religion so effects one possessing it that they must not laugh, but must always look pious and grave. When the emotions are excited because of expecting or receiving something good it is hardly probable that one will all the time look sober and grave, but will at least show something else at times. The Apostle Paul takes up the same theme, and writes: "Rejoice evermore," (1 Thes. 5:16) as if there was some reason for it, and something to be gained by such an experience. ,

After the one hundred and twenty had received the baptism with the Holy Ghost, and had spoken in tongues as the Spirit gave utterance; and after the three thousand had received the same experience and were added to them, they all "continued steadfastly in the apostles' doctrine and fellowship; * *   and they continuing daily with one accord in the temple, and breaking bread from house to house, did eat their meat with GLADNESS and singleness of heart, praising God and having

favor with all the people. And the Lord added to
the church daily such as should be saved." These
are some of the results of obeying the words of Jesus, and by so doing did not only result in themselves getting the joy, but many, many others besides.

Happiness is constantly sought for by the multitudes, but how few there are that have learned
the secret of obtaining it. The words of Jesus
were spoken so people would know how to obtain
the experience that would naturally produce that
happiness or joy. Obedience to the words of Jesus
will put people into that very state where they can
rejoice and be exceeding glad when they are re-
viled, persecuted, and their names cast out as evil.
How few even good people have arrived at that
state of experience!

The companions of the bride are to be brought
with gladness and rejoicing, and they shall enter into
the King's palace. (Ps. 45:15.) And if the companions of the bride will be brought with such rejoicing, how much more joy will be realized by the
bride herself!

There is something in this joy and rejoicing of
great value, or surely the writers of the Bible would
not have emphasized it so much. The psalmist
sang, "We will rejoice in thy salvation and in the
name of our God we will set up our banners." De-

light thyself also in the Lord; and he shall give thee the desires of thine heart."

When Nehemiah found his people weeping and mourning as they listened to the reading of the law, he urged them to refrain from weeping, for said he, "The joy of the Lord is your strength." While weeping may be in order at times, yet it should not be continued; for it is the joy of the Lord that gives strength. "Weeping may endure for a night, but joy cometh in the morning." "They that sow in tears shall reap in joy. He that goeth forth and weepeth, bearing precious seed, shall doubtless come again with rejoicing, bringing his sheaves with him."

It has been said that "A sad Christian is always a weak Christian. God never sends a discouraged person to help some one who is discouraged." People have enough sadness, they want joy. Be a cheerful, joyous Christian, and you will be wanted and appreciated. There is enough gloom in the world. Turn it into gladness and joy by being a happy sparkling Christian yourself. To look sad and dejected causes a pang to pierce the heart of your companion or those with whom you mingle. Get the experience that obedience to Jesus' words will put into you, and you will be successful in helping others.

Think of Jesus, "A man of sorrows, and acquainted with grief," and on His way to the judgment hall a crown of thorns, a scourging and final crucifixion, talking about joy.   But it was a pleasure to Him to do His Father's will, for He said, "My meat is to do the will of him that hath sent me, and to finish his work."   It must have been to Him a source of great joy to approach such a crisis, for He said to His disciples the very night He was arrested, when He was telling them of His departure, which caused them sorrow and pain, "If ye loved me, ye would rejoice, because I said, I go unto my Father."

It has often been said of Pentecostal people: "They are the happiest people I ever saw, and their faces seem to shine with the radiance of heaven." Many doubters and unbelievers have been convinced by the shine on the face of some who talked in tongues under the power of God.   A writer says: "Pentecostal joy is often uncontainable, inexpressible.   Its possession often causes the possessor to be grievously misunderstood, for he laughs when others would weep, he sings when others would sigh, he shouts when others would sulk and pout, he dances when the heavens are black with disappointment.   When his heart is filled with unutterable sorrow, he smiles even through his tears!   He is never offended.   Indeed it is sometimes said of him that he does not know enough to know when he is insulted.   This latter is certainly a blissful ignorance."

Jesus was anointed "with the oil of gladness" above His fellows, and he is the leader of that happy band who shall "come to Zion with songs of everlasting joy upon their heads," who "shall obtain joy and gladness, and sorrow and sighing shall flee away."

At creation's dawn "the morning stars sang together," and until sin came and all was marred by its cruel insult, joy and gladness reigned supremely everywhere. Jesus came to redeem us from the fall, and when lifted back to edenic innocency by His supernal power the Holy Ghost restores to us the joy that was lost. We never think of combining salvation and melancholy.

A house was wrapped in flames. A fireman was vainly endeavoring to reach an upper window where a precious little child was gasping for breath. He was almost despairing, when some one in the crowd shouted out, "Cheer him," and from a thousand throats went up a shout of encouragement, and the arm strengthened, the head was cleared and the man dashed through the smoke and flame and rescued the precious child. How much more should we be so possessed with His joy and rejoicing that we can shout and cheer each other along in an attempt to rescue immortal souls from the flames of hell-fire!

We are told that there are great corporations and

business enterprises in this country which will not employ a man if he is known to be unhappy in domestic relationships. His services are worth more if he is happy in his home. Now, if joy is at such a premium in secular things, how much more in God's service! God wants happy people in His service. Those who are free from the "blues." A happy victorious people, who can bring sunshine in place of shadow. God is seeking a people who will engage in this last great conflict gladly and joyfully. And if persecution or trouble comes upon them (and it will come), they can be like the disciples. "And they departed from the presence of the council, rejoicing that they were counted worthy to suffer shame for his name." (Acts 5:41.)

With a few men and women that fear nothing but God, and who are filled with the joy of Jesus and possessed with that fullness of joy, God can accomplish great things even in our day. One of the greatest hindrances to the work and spread of the gospel is the talk and murmur proceeding from people who are slightly "soured." They will use language that will have a tendency to discourage those who would otherwise go on. One person, who is a "fault-finder" and without this glad victorious joy, can wreck more lives and hinder the advancement of God's cause more than a dozen sinners. Joy, victorious joy, is a jewel that every child of God ought to carry, and an ornament that should be displayed at every corner and avenue of life. It is an armour that every soldier enlisted in this last great conflict should have strapped tight upon him.

If Stephen's face could shine like the face of an angel in the midst of a volley of stones as they were hurled down upon him, why not your face shine while in the common walks of life? I have seen dear Christian? friends, with apparently nothing to cause it, live such miserable lives that they would cause a shadow and groan of distress to enter the hearts of all who mingled with them. There is certainly a place in the center of God's will where the sun will shine through the densest clouds. "Hope maketh not ashamed."

There is a great need for strong men and women in the Master's service. The joy of the Lord—His joy—fullness of joy, will give the needed strength. This joy can be obtained by perfect obedience to Jesus.

Look up, dear dejected soul, and receive a refreshing shower from above. Discouragement comes from the enemy of your soul. There is no need of living so far beneath your privileges, and it is your privilege to have His joy, and your joy made full. Pray and look up. Take hold of your possessions. It is yours through Jesus. Hallelujah! "Rejoice in the Lord alway: and again I say, Rejoice."

In the experience of St. Andrew is given an example of joy and happiness in the hour of the most cruel treatment. Aegenas first ordered him to be scourged, seven lictors successively whipping his naked body; and seeing his invincible patience and constancy, commanded him to be crucified; but to be fastened to the X like cross with cords instead of nails, that his death might be more lingering and tedious. As he was led to the place of execution, walking with a cheerful and composed mind, the people cried out, that a good and innocent man was unjustly condemned to die. On his coming near the cross, he saluted it in the following manner: "I have long desired and expected this happy hour. The cross has been consecrated by the body of Christ hanging on it, and adorned with his members as with so many inestimable jewels. I therefore come joyfully and triumphantly to it, that it may receive me as a disciple and follower of Him who once hung upon it, and be the means of carrying me safe to my Master, being the instrument on which He redeemed me." After offering up his prayers to a throne of grace, and exhorting the people to constancy and perseverance in the faith he had delivered to them, he was fastened to the cross, on which he hung two whole days, teaching and instructing the people.

CHAPTER VI.

CHRIST OUR LAW-GIVER.

There are a number of people who have enjoyed the "latter rain" showers that have been falling, and who have received the baptism with the Holy Ghost, but are floating around as a sailing vessel which has no chart or compass. Their sails are spread, and as the wind blows in a certain direction they move off with great joy and liberty; but when that puff of wind ceases and another one comes from another direction, off they go again with that gust, though it may be driving them almost in an opposite course. Just so they are sailing, they seem to be satisfied.

Sailors with a chart and compass for a guide will hoist their sails and fly before the wind, provided it carries them the way they wish to travel, but when the wind comes that is contrary they either take down their sails and anchor or shift them and tack until a more favorable breeze comes again.

We should not be carried about by every wind of doctrine. It is very unsatisfactory to be unsettled. One who is unsettled is unsafe, and one who is settled on the wrong foundation is also dangerous. It is always good for a man to change from the wrong to the right, but it is very serious to change from the right to the wrong.

I have in mind a sweet Christian character who was very strong against a certain line of truth, but in a short time the tempest seemed to blow so hard in the right direction, that the precious soul was driven by the tempest and accepted the truth, but he remains so unsettled, judging from his conversation, that there are some fears that if he was to get into a severe tempest beating against this same line of truth, he would fall in with that tempest and turn in the opposite direction again. We cannot trust such a person, neither can God depend upon him. Rooted and grounded in the truth is the only safe place.

The question is often asked, "What should the Pentecostal people do as pertaining to organization? Should they organize, or remain with no order or government?" There is only one way to settle these questions, and that is to examine the Scriptures unbiased and without prejudice. Not only should the whole "latter rain" affection be ONE in answer to the prayer of Jesus, but all real Christians ought to be joined together in one body. "Now I beseech you, brethren, by the name of our Lord Jesus Christ, that ye all speak the same thing, and that there be no divisions among you; but that ye be perfectly joined together in the same mind, and in the same judgment." (1 Cor. 1:10.) "Fulfill ye my joy, that ye may be like-minded, having the same love, being of one accord, of one mind." (Phil. 2:2.) Two or more minds might run together and they agree on something that was wrong, and for fear that this might be the case, and as if in order to cut off occasion for such a serious error, Paul adds, "Let this mind be in you, which was also in Christ Jesus." (Phil. 2:5.) This then is intended to put us in one accord with Christ, and if all the followers and disciples of Jesus Christ are in accord with Him they will be in one accord with each other as a whole.

What should the Christian people do? Get in perfect harmony and one accord with Christ in spirit, mind and teaching, and this will bring us to-either into one body, one organization, under one, government, with one law-giver—Christ—who is the head of the church. Jesus instituted His Church for government, and all the laws for government came from Him to us through His holy apostles.

I admit that we have those in our ranks who oppose government and any form of organization, but such are false teachers. They refuse to submit to government, and are holding themselves aloof and independent, every one for himself, even contending against any form of organization, and say they are members of Christ's church. It matters not how spiritual they may seem to be, or how honest

they may be, they are dangerous characters, and
enemies to Christ and His truth: "But there were
false prophets also among the people, even as there
shall be false teachers among you, who privily shall
bring in damnable heresies, even denying the Lord
* * * * and despise government. Presump-
tuous are they, self willed, they are not afraid to
speak evil of dignities." (2 Peter 2;1, 10.) "Likewise also these filthy dreamers defile the flesh, despise dominion (government), and speak evil of dignities." (Jude 8.) No one can be a member of
Christ's church and refuse government and hold
themselves aloof from organization—His organization—His government—His laws.

His Church means government. It is not a legis-
lative or law making body, but an executive body.
It executes the laws already given. It is also a ju-
dicial body, because it applies the laws already en-
acted to particular cases. To object to dominion, to
despise government, to refuse organization means
opposition to the council at Jerusalem (Acts 15), and
means opposition to Christ's church.

His church for the saints in this world is what His
kingdom is to be universally in the millennium. If
we prove ourselves to be good executives here, we
will more likely receive a kingdom over which to
reign there. If we prove ourselves obedient to His
laws here and now He will more likely trust us

with the reins of government there and then.

In the teaching of the parable of the pounds given by our Lord (Luke 19:12-27), He shows the value of obedience and faithfulness to His government and laws, and in verse 27 He calls the people His enemies who refuse His reigning over them, commanding them to be brought and slain before Him. If I reject His government and disobey His laws, I make myself a disloyal subject, and according to this teaching I must be slain.

The Apostle Paul gives the same teaching at 2 Thes. 1:7-9, where he says—"The Lord Jesus shall be revealed from heaven with His mighty angels, in flaming fire, taking vengeance on them that know not God, and that obey not the gospel (commands) of our Lord Jesus Christ: who shall be punished with everlasting destruction from the presence of the Lord, and from the glory of His power." The reading of this Scripture calls for another to explain what it is to obey God, for we read here that He is going to take vengeance on them that do not obey Him. At 1 John 2:3, 4, we are told of a proof for our knowing Him. "And hereby we do know that we know him, if we keep his commandments. He that saith, I know him, and keepeth not his commandments, is a liar, and the truth is not in him." These Scriptures surely ought to teach every one the importance of perfect obedience to His laws.

We frequently hear people say "I know I have
passed from death unto life because I love the brethren," which is a quotation of I John 3:14, which
is all right, but let us look a little farther on and see
what it is to love God's children or the brethren.
"By this we know that we love the children of God
(brethren), when we love God, and keep his commandments. For this is the love of God, that we
keep his commandments." This brings us down to
obedience to His laws and government again.
Christ's laws. Christ's government.

"God, who at sundry times and in divers manners
spake in time past unto the fathers by the prophets,
hath in these last days spoken unto us by his Son."
(Heb. 1:1, 2.) Then to be loyal subjects of His government, we must obey His laws or commands.
We have already shown that to refuse to do this,
makes us worthy of being slain or punished with
everlasting destruction.

Many people to-day who claim to be members of
Christ's Church (government), remind me of people
who come from foreign countries to the United States
and fail to take the "oath of allegiance." They are
on United States soil or territory, reaping the benefits therefrom, but not United States citizens. Israel was recognized by God as His children and
chosen people, but not until they crossed the Red
sea and accepted and covenanted to keep the laws

of God given them through Moses were they recognized as, or called the "Church in the wilderness."

Church then means government—Christ's government: His Church. Here then is where women
are to keep silence. that is, they are to have no active part in the governmental affairs. (1 Cor. 14:34.)
Here, too, is where Paul said he would rather speak
five words with his understanding that with his voice
he might teach others, than ten thousand words
with an unknown tongue. (1 Cor. 14:19.) Here,
also, is where not over three at most, and they one
at a time, may speak in tongues and let one interpret, and if there be no interpreter let him keep
silent in the church. (1 Cor. 14:27, 28.) There
were no women speaking in the council at Jerusalem: no one talking in tongues. They were a judi-
cial body, searching for and applying the laws to a
particular case. When the law was found touching
that particular case it was applied, and James, who
seemed to be chairman or moderator, made the
statement which settled all discussion and debate,
and there were no votes taken because they only
had to obey the law already given, and only added
words of explanation.

His Church is not a government by the people,
which is democratic form, neither is it government
by the people by representatives, which is republi-

can form; but "The government shall be upon his shoulder." (Isa. 9:6.) His church is a theocracy. God giving His laws through Moses is a type. God giving His laws through Christ is evidently the antitype and very image—the perfection for government. "For the law having a shadow of good things to come and not the very image of the things." (Heb. 10:1.) This signifies that Christ's is the real government of which Moses' was only a shadow. The government through Moses has had an end, but the government under Christ is to continue—perpetuate. "Of the increase of His government * * * * there shall be no end." (Isa. 9:7.)

He is to rule or govern His church in this world' as Moses governed Israel in the wilderness. As Israel was a peculiar treasure unto God among thousands of inhabitants, but separate from them, so Christ "gave himself for us, that he might redeem us from all iniquity, and purify unto himself a peculiar people, zealous of good works." (Titus 2:14.)

We are in the world but not of the world. We are under Christ's government, but must be subject to "the powers that be" in whatever country we are placed, except the world governments conflict with our obligations to Christ. Then Christ must be honored and obeyed rather than the world governments even at the peril of our lives. (Acts 4:19; 5:29.)

"Christ is the head of the church: and he is the

savior of the body." Therefore the church is to be
subject to Him in everything. "Christ also loved
the church, and gave himself for it; That he might
sanctify and cleanse it with the washing of water
by the word, that he might present it to himself a
glorious church, not having spot, or wrinkle, or any
such thing; but that it should be holy and without
blemish." (Eph. 5:23-27.) Those then who have
followed and obeyed Him faithfully here will con-
stitute His great host of rulers and governors during
His thousand years reign on earth, when He shall
reign without a rival. All people and all nations
will be subject unto Him. "And the Lord God shall
give unto him the throne of his father David: * *
* * And of his kingdom there shall be no end."
(Luke 1:32, 33.)

CHAPTER VII.

FELLOWSHIP OF THE MYSTERY.

That the people of God need a much deeper and broader experience is evident. It is also true and clear to the intelligent spiritual observer that God has provided for a much deeper experience in the atonement. It is a fact that the Lord's children are living far beneath their privilege in Christ.

If the above statements are true, then every honest, humble, trusting child of God should not only pray and press his way toward the prize offered him, but should plunge into the great realm of grace deeper and yet deeper until the promised prize is obtained. Not only should this greater and deeper experience be sought after and possessed for the benefit of the seeker, but all should remember that more souls could be saved from eternal destruction by His followers receiving from God this deeper experience.

The deep water is not disturbed by the surface winds. Then there is no time to tarry at the surface, for souls are swiftly going down to eternal despair. To remain at the surface means to take too much time to battle with the surface winds, which are a detriment to your progress. While you are hindered by such forces in your own experience, you are not able to do what you otherwise could if you were deeper down, where the external disturbances would have no effect on you or disturb you while engaged in rescuing precious souls that would otherwise be lost.

A deeper experience means a more forcible and powerful experience. As the earth is firmer beneath the surface, and the water more dense, so with one's experience. One who has this deep experience and is firm, is less apt to be driven about and tossed to and fro with every wind of doctrine, therefore he is more able to win souls to Christ. To be settled and established in the wrong place is indeed very serious; but to be established and fastened in the right place, as "a nail driven in a sure place," with an eye and determination to search the very depths of the Christian experience that was wrought for humanity in Christ is indeed a precious treasure.

As the value of souls is so great, and their salvation so important as to call for such a sacrifice as was made at Calvary to redeem them, then surely we ought to see and feel the importance of deepening our experience, if by doing so will be the means of rescuing more of them. If the value of souls and the extension and spread of the gospel of Jesus Christ were of such consequence as to call men abruptly from their occupation, as was the case with Jesus' disciples, can we think the value of the same has decreased since that time? Nay, verily, there is no fluctuation of prices and values of souls as there is in the products of this world. If we judge by the appearance to-day in comparison with the appearance in the days of Jesus and His disciples, we would readily conclude values and prices of souls have decreased, for who ever hears of one in these days dropping and suspending business at the call of God as Peter the fisherman and Matthew the tax collector? Who ever hears of one hundred and twenty in one place forsaking everything of this world and gathering together for a deepening of experience, for an indefinite period of time, as the disciples and others did in the early years of the gospel dispensation? And this, too, that they might be more effective in soul saving.

This is surely a time for people who claim to love Jesus and souls to awake, and remember the value and price of souls is the same now as then, and get a deeper experience, not only to prepare themselves for the meeting in the air, but for the salvation of souls as well. It is as important for "this gospel of the kingdom" to be preached in all the world now as then. It is as important to rescue souls now as then.

The Holy Ghost is given for service and not for pleasure. He is to guide into all truth, even into the fellowship of the mystery. The natural man cannot comprehend the things of God, but "the Spirit

searcheth all things, yea, the deep things of God."
Then if you have Him dwelling in your mortal body
you may expect to be led deeper and yet deeper
until the end is reached. To receive the Holy Ghost
and not go deeper than when you received Him is
to backslide, the Spirit become grieved, and you become hard and tough in your experience and dissat-
isfied with yourself and everybody else. The Holy
Ghost is to guide you into all truth, which indicates
a constant moving forward toward the goal.

I am now on the steamship Miami out on the wa-
ters of the broad Atlantic, and the pilot is on board.
As the large vessel moves forward he does the guiding, and if she keeps moving forward he will guide
her safely into port; but if her engines should stop,
and thus she become lifeless in the midst of the sea,
the pilot will be unable to accomplish his purpose.
So with the Holy Ghost as our Pilot. As long as we
keep moving forward He will guide, but if we stop
He is unable to accomplish His purpose in our lives.
But as we keep moving on He will plunge us deeper
into the mysteries of God wrought out for us in the
sacrifice and atonement made on Calvary. "He
that spared not his own Son, but delivered him up
for us all, how shall he not with him also freely give
us all things?" (Rom. 8:32.) Wonderful promise,
but true, and He that promised is faithful. God cannot deny Himself. But in order to reach the goal

and obtain the prize we must keep moving on, so
our Pilot can guide us safe into port.   Glory!

As we keep moving on and on we get farther and
farther into the unknown. But we must not shrink nor
fear.   Move on with confidence, and don't be afraid
of getting beside yourself.   Don't be uneasy about
fanaticism.   Move on and He will guide, and if He
guides you are safe.   And if He guides into all truth
He is sure to guide you out of all error, so you have
nothing to fear.

As you get deeper and deeper you will lose the
fellowship of the world and will soon have a sweet
fellowship with something that has hitherto been unknown. The veil of separation was rent from top'
to bottom, and now we have the wonderful privilege
of going softly into the chamber where we can have
the fellowship of the mystery (Eph. 3:9), that has
been long hidden from man.   It is now high time for
God's dear children and humble followers to make
a dive for the deeper and unexplored regions beyond, which He purposed in Christ for us before
the world was.   (Eph. 3:11.)

These deeper things and experiences are to be
sought for and obtained and realized by the church.
A fellowship of the mystery; a familiar intercourse
with principalities; a partnership with powers. (Eph
3:10.) Wonderful! Glorious in the extreme! Such
as this granted to man! But where are we? Tossed

about by external forces, instead of going into the depths beyond. It is high time for us to strain ourselves to the very utmost if need be, and bring every nerve into use, if it takes that, and move on into that which was purchased for us and rightfully belongs to us. If WE don't go on and possess these high attainments somebody ELSE WILL. God is going to accomplish His purpose.

There has been a time for deep thought. That time is now past. We are now to pass the zenith of thought and try the untrodden path of mystery. Don't get scared now as you read. Keep looking up, and move on. If your Pilot is on board you have nothing to fear. He is always delighted to have you increase your speed. He is able for emergency calls. He will never fail you if you fully trust Him. You may think sometimes you are going contrary to good judgment; but you are going right if He is guiding. He wants to get you to the place where you "May be able to comprehend with all saints what is the breadth, and length, and depth, and height; and to know the love of Christ which passeth knowledge that ye might be filled with all the fullness of God." (Eph. 3:18, 19.)

This deep experience; this fellowship of the mystery; this familiar intercourse with principalities and powers in heavenly places; yea, this being filled with all the fullness of God is not too much to expect

through Him who went to Calvary to obtain for us
this wonderful experience: for He is able to do for
us "exceeding abundantly above all that we ask or
think, according to the power that worketh in us."
(Eph. 3:20.)

In conclusion I wish to impress on the hearts and
minds of the precious people who read these pages
the importance of this subject. Much depends on
each one of you in these days of the last great conflict. That the world must have the gospel given
them is evident. That it never will be done by the
plans now in vogue is also evident, for it is said that
while in the last one hundred years there have been
two millions reached, there has been an increase of
heathens of two hundred millions during the same
period of time. It is an acknowledged fact that
NEW plans must be discovered and inaugurated.
Then we must resort to another source for plans,
and the only sure source for fully developed plans,
and those which, if followed, will bring success and
victory, are to be found only in His Word; and to
accept His plans fully means a deeper and yet
deeper experience that will take us away from the
common to the unknown; from the natural to the
supernatural and from the human to the divine. This
and this only will carry the gospel into all the world
for a witness in this generation.

Long study and deep thought have been a comparative failure.   Again I wish to say, It is time now to pass beyond the zenith of deep tiresome thinking and enter the secret vaults of the mystery of revelation.   A real experience must first be obtained; then "Go!" fired up with holy zeal and undaunted courage, and the power will work in you mightily as He guides you on to certain victory.   Be sure and move on into this deeper experience for the glory of God and the advancement of the cause you love so well!   The full benefits to the atonement are ours if we will only appropriate them to our use for the glory of God and the salvation of a lost world.

CHAPTER VIII.

LOOKING FORWARD

Within the nature and the makeup of man there is a tendency to look back and recount the things of the past. This may not be wrong, however, as in many cases one is better able to see what is to come by a careful study of the things of the past; but there have been many backward glances which have proved detrimental to the progress of the traveler, and in some instances even fatal.

When Lot and his wife and two daughters were leaving the city of Sodom, hurried away by the two angels and commanded by them not to look back, Mrs. Lot failed to take heed to the command, and turned her head and looked behind, and immediately she was turned into a pillar of salt, and Jesus said, "Remember Lot's wife."

When Israel was marching from Egypt to the promised land, not a few longed to turn back to the flesh-pots and other things they had left behind; and with Core at the head as leader of quite a number, they were about to start back when the earth opened and swallowed them up.

General Gideon started out to battle with thirty-two thousand soldiers, but twenty-two thousand turned back because they were fearful and faint-hearted. Soon nine thousand and seven hundred more went back because they proved themselves unfit for service. There were only three hundred of that large army of men that were so zealous and occupied with the laurels of conquest and victory ahead, that proved themselves fit and able for the required service.

Multitudes had been following Jesus, but when He began to teach them the great and deep spiritual truths they pronounced them "hard sayings," became offended in Him and went back and never followed Him any more. At that time only the twelve were left with Him. After His resurrection, Paul states that He was seen by about five hundred brethren at one time, but only about one hundred and twenty were noted as being in the upper room on the day of Pentecost.

At the time of the rapture a multitude (represented by the five foolish virgins of Math. 25) will be left behind because of the looking backward tendency in their lives, until they have made the final fatal mistake because of not pressing forward.

Jesus said, "No man, having put his hand to the plough, and looking back, is fit for the kingdom of God." The writer of Hebrews says, "If any man draw back, my soul shall have no pleasure in him." Paul said, "This one thing I do, forgetting those things which are behind, and reaching forth unto those things which are before, I press toward the mark for the prize of the high calling of God in Christ Jesus. Let us therefore, as many as be perfect, be thus minded. * * * * Nevertheless, whereunto we have already attained let us walk by the same rule, let us mind the same thing." "Neither give heed to fables and endless genealogies, which minister questions, rather than godly edifying." "But avoid foolish questions and strivings about the law; for they are unprofitable and vain."

I was once running from a vicious animal, and I never looked back to see if the animal was following until I reached a place of safety. Had I looked back I might have stumbled and fallen and been overtaken. A story is told of a little fellow who had fallen and bruised himself; on being asked how it happened he said, "I was a runnin' and lookin' back, and come to a high place in the ground and I fell."

We are indeed running a race, and the prize is at the end of the race. To look back and cavil over Old Testament Scriptures, or to stop and cavil over anything, endangers us so we may fall in the race. Indeed, we should study the Scriptures, but to take time to go back and try to decipher some of the mysteries that belonged to the past ages, and thus raise an argument and wound the feelings of precious souls, instead of edifying and blessing them, is

a loss of time, to say nothing of how we ourselves
might fall in the race while looking back.

The prophets of old were looking forward. The
reason they saw far ahead was because they were
looking in that direction. "Of which salvation the
prophets have enquired and searched diligently,
who prophesied of the grace that should come unto
you: Searching what, or what manner of time the
Spirit of Christ which was in them did signify, when
it testified before hand the sufferings of Christ, and
the glory that should follow." (1 Peter 1:10, 11.)
And as they searched, the truth of the matter was
revealed unto them. They were looking forward,
and the revelation was given unto them.

A true prophet is looking ahead, and if he is looking forward he will have enough to engage him
without striving or debating about things of the past.
As I write and become inspired with the subject,
and my mind goes leaping and bounding over the
hills and plains of the future, a faint voice seems to
be heard in the distance, which finally bursts forth
in a loud tone and utters words that are almost startling, "Look ahead, and not behind."

It has been estimated that one hundred thousand
persons have received the baptism with the Holy
Ghost, evidenced by the speaking in tongues as the
Spirit gave utterance, in the last four years. We
hear of many apparently wearying in the race and

drawing back, but hundreds are pressing on after the gifts, power and glory, realizing that there is a great plenty before to interest and occupy them without spending too much time in looking back.

Men are searching and counting and spending their time with prophecies and figures trying to ascertain about the time of the end of the age, the catching away of the saints to meet the Lord in the air, and the revelation of the antichrist, etc., etc. They are making chronology a special study and producing drawings and figures and fixing dates and times for the transpiring of certain events, merely from the study of Scriptures and books. I do not say this is wrong, but probably in connection with the searching a nearer and better way to ascertain this knowledge would be to court the favor of God and the fellowship of the mystery (Eph. 3:9), and the deeper spiritual experiences that are obtainable through Christ until, like the prophets of old, it will be revealed.

"Surely the Lord will do nothing, but He revealeth His secret unto His servants the prophets." (Amos 3:7.) He would not destroy Sodom without talking to Abraham about it. "But of the times and the seasons, brethren, ye have no need that I write unto you. For yourselves know perfectly that the day of the Lord so cometh as a thief in the night. For when they shall say, Peace and safety; then sudden destruction cometh upon them, as travail upon a woman with child; and they shall not escape. But ye, brethren, are not in darkness, that that day should overtake you as a thief. Ye are all the children of light, and the children of the day: We are not of the night nor of darkness." (1 Thes. 5:1-5.)

Again I say, we have plenty to occupy us without caviling or disputing over things of the past. These are tremendous days. Days of great privilege: days of conquest. Our time should be spent in forming a closer fellowship with God and the Celestial beings. There is a realm in which we can remain similar to that in which Enoch and Elijah dwelt. Experience and revelation are far better than mere intellectual knowledge. The prophets searched, but by and by the revelation was given them.

The three wise men saw the star and thus traveled together until they actually saw the Christ. If we keep our eyes and minds fixed on the Ideal Life (Jesus), we can certainly travel together, and will be so occupied with what the future will disclose that there will be no time for looking back and caviling over things of the past. Paul said, "Forgetting the things behind" because the things before are more inspiring and interesting. Hallelujah! We have had the past, we now enjoy the present, but the future, Oh how glorious! And it is so near at hand: within our reach.

We have had sermonizing and great preaching,
but that is so common. We have the experiences
of justification, sanctification and the baptism with
the Holy Ghost. We have the tongues (not the
gift) given by the Spirit. We must not and do not
depreciate the value of preaching nor of the tongues,
but the gifts and great power that are obtainable are
yet to come.

Peter went throughout all quarters, and when he
came to the house of Aeneas where he lay sick, a
few words from Peter and sickness vanished, and
Aeneas was well. When he entered the place
where Dorcas lay a corpse, a short prayer and a
few words from Peter, and she was alive. The
signs and wonders were so numerous, producing
such a sensation that the multitudes were stirred and
agitated continually. How the gospel flew over the
then known world! Not in word only, but in power
and demonstration of the Spirit. It was sensational,
but glorious results followed.

They are trying to hold us down with what little
we now have, but the future, what will it descry?
What will it reveal? What running to and fro carrying the sick, halt and lame, and all will be healed!
Who are going to be the manifest sons of God for
which the whole creation is waiting? This is just
ahead. See them as they walk triumphantly amid
demons, contagious diseases and persecutions. Look

at them as they walk victoriously into the insane asylums and drive out the legions of demons and set the captives free. See them as they enter the hospitals, infirmaries, deaf and dumb asylums and pest houses and so relieve the inmates that these homes for the afflicted will be turned into pentecostal chambers and the superintendents and overseers will stand and look on with amazement and wonder.

Look into the future! What does it mean to you? Have you any time to draw back? Have you the time to even look back? Can you afford to take your eyes and mind off the future glory and triumphant, overwhelming, stupendous conquests and victories long enough to parley, debate or cavil over things of the past? Have you any time to hold a grudge, malice, envy or hatred? Do you have time to back-bite, or carry tales, or handle reproaches against your neighbors or your brothers and sisters in the church? Are you willing for others to get ahead of you in spirituality and spiritual things?

Do you want to stop and cavil over some theories and petty notions, and by doing this let others get so far ahead of you in the race that they will enter the land of visions and revelations, and converse with angels, principalities and other celestial beings while you are left behind to grope your way with the multitudes who are in the dark?

Just a little space, and somebody is going to pass over into 2 Cor. 12:12. "Truly the signs of an apostle were wrought among you in all patience, in signs, and wonders, and mighty deeds." Do you have any aspiration to attain to such a height of glory and power? If so you are one that is looking forward, and not behind. If you aspire to these tremendous realms of grace, glory and power you are so occupied and interested that you have no time to spend in the out of date things of the past, only as you use them as stepping stones to higher heights, thus putting them beneath your feet, and as Paul said, "Forgetting those things which are behind," and busy yourself with "reaching forth unto those things which are before."

Oh, glorious achievement! Oh, magazine of power! Oh, humility and love! Oh, great arm of the Lord! We bid you welcome to step in and take control and begin to perform the exploits due to our generation.

CHAPTER IX.

Ever since the transgression and fall of man the human body has been subject to disease. The human race has been tortured with pain and misery, and harassed with loathsome diseases in all ages since Adam and Eve were driven outside the beautiful garden of Eden. No doubt our foreparents died in ignorance of what they had brought on their posterity by that one act of disobedience.

That little innocent child lying there on that downy pillow scorching with fever; those plaintive moans and groans that grate upon the mother's heart and rasp her very life chords like the knife of an army surgeon upon his victim: those sweet little weak eyes that follow mamma as she moves about the room, as if pleading with her for relief, tells the story and paints the picture of thousands of homes made unhappy by the transgression that plunged the entire human race into a dilemma of dire diseases.

You ask why the poverty of that home, as you pass by the clapboard shanty by the wayside. Ah! if you only knew of the sleepless nights of watching over husband while he was pining away, not only from the torture of some dread disease, but the application of his mind as he knew his family were being rapidly reduced to poverty because he was not able to attend to his business and earn an honest living for his faithful wife and little innocent children, you would hardly dare ask such a question.

Families in good circumstances have often been reduced to poverty because of one blow after another by some dread disease. Happiness and comfort have given way year by year to sadness, discouragement, despair and penury, until they could hardly be recognized as the same happy, prosperous family of a few years ago. In vain have they paid out their hard earned money for physicians and remedies. They are down, with but little hope of rising again.

While poverty and discouragement have overtaken many, many homes, and they have gone from one cheap house to a cheaper one on account of it, look for a moment upon that beautiful mansion yonder among the trees. "O, isn't that magnificent?" you say. "That belongs to Dr. ————." I need not say any more, you know the story. Physicians rise to prominence and wealth, while their patients and patrons take the road in the opposite direction. As one physician goes up in the scale of wealth a dozen or more families are reduced to poverty.

We have had pointed out to us the stately mansions of the saloon keepers on the one hand and the poor drunkard in the ditch on the other as an argument in favor of temperance and prohibition. We do not criticise the argument, but rather wish to endorse it, and if possible make it stronger, but we cannot afford to strain that argument and entirely cover up and neglect the same argument in regard to drugs, medicines, druggists and physicians. I do not need to point out to you the thousands of wealthy druggists and physicians made so by the ill fate of the millions of unfortunates who have doped themselves with pills and patent medicines.

While you are studying over these matters let God come on the scene, and you listen as He speaks: "But it shall come to pass, if thou wilt not hearken unto the voice of the Lord thy God, to observe to do all his commandments and his statutes which I command thee * * * * the Lord shall send upon thee cursing, vexation and rebuke, in all that thou settest thine hand unto for to do, until thou be destroyed, and until thou perish quickly; because of the wickedness of thy doings, whereby thou hast forsaken me. The Lord shall make the pestilence cleave unto thee, * * * * the Lord shall smite thee with consumption, and with a fever, and with an inflammation, and with an extreme burning. * *
* * The Lord will smite thee with the botch of Egypt, and with the emerods, and with the scab and with itch, whereof thou canst not be healed, *
* * * and thou shalt not prosper in thy ways;

and thou shalt be only oppressed and spoiled ever-more, and no man shall save thee." "In vain shalt thou use many medicines; for thou shalt not be cured."

In the face of these Scriptures people go right on and pay out their money and make druggists and physicians wealthy, instead of resorting to God's way for healing. The ministers are not a little to blame, for they fail to preach and teach God's way of healing, and set the example by resorting to medical aid themselves when they get sick. The custom has grown so strong that it is almost impossible to break away from it, but the truth of God's Word will stand if everybody goes down.

What advantage is it to you to invest your money in palaces and palatial residences for somebody else to occupy when God says their medicines will not cure you? Are their medicines stronger than God's Word? Are you going to continue to heap up condemnation and disobedience on yourself by resorting to physicians and medicine contrary to God's Word? Indeed they are legislating against God and His Word, but His Word will stand when their legislations are hurled into the lake of fire, where they themselves are plowing the billows of an endless eternity.

Let us now turn away from this picture and look at another more beautiful, more pleasant, which gives more encouragement and higher aspirations. There are many good people who believe God is able to heal their diseases in answer to prayer that have not been able to see healing in the atonement the same as salvation for the soul.

It is our purpose to make a few statements and give some Scriptures bearing on the subject for the consideration of those who may be interested, with a desire to encourage the faith of all who may read these pages.

In Psalms 103:2, 3, please read: "Bless the Lord, O my soul, and forget not all his benefits: Who forgiveth all thine iniquities; who healeth all thy diseases." The Psalmist here indicates that although we might forget some of the Lord's benefits to us, we should not forget these: that God forgives our sins and heals our bodies.

The human race have largely forgotten these two benefits, and even many professed Christians have forgotten both, yet more, probably, have forgotten the latter than the former. It is surely strange that people are so forgetful of things that pertain to their own interests. No doubt there are many today in poverty and sadness who would have been in good health and had plenty of home comforts if they had only remembered God's way of healing. They could have given their money to God's cause and had an increase by so doing, instead of investing it in fine houses and furniture, carriages and automobiles for druggists and physicians to revel in, and reduced themselves to poverty thereby.

The Bible is, or could be in every home in America, and yet people are so occupied with the things of the world that they are unmindful of the good things contained therein that ought to be remembered for the good of themselves. They buy doctor books and search them through and through for symptoms and remedies, while the Bible lies unopened and unused, except occasionally on Sunday, when their consciences get to lashing them heavily, after reading the Sunday newspapers nearly all day.

In Isa. 53, the atonement chapter, the prophet did not speak only of salvation of the soul, but healing for the body as well. Verses 4 and 5 should be read and studied carefully. "Surely he hath borne our griefs and carried our sorrows: yet we did esteem him stricken, smitten of God and afflicted. But he was wounded for our transgressions, he was bruised for our iniquities: the chastisement of our peace was upon him; and with his stripes (bruise—margin) we are healed." This same Scripture is mentioned in Math. 8:16, 17. "When the even was come, they brought unto him (Jesus) many that were possessed with devils; and he cast out the spirits with his word, and healed all that were sick: That it might be fulfilled which was spoken by Esaias (Isaiah) the prophet, saying, Himself took our infirmities and bare our sicknesses."

There are many good people to-day who believe God has power to heal, and will and does heal in answer to prayer, that never think of healing being provided for them in the atonement the same as salvation for the soul. When people see this fully it will no doubt inspire more faith for healing. Indeed there is no other way provided, as shown in the Bible, for salvation except by and through Jesus Christ. And there is no other way provided for the healing of the body except through Jesus Christ. To resort to other means and remedies is to transgress and disobey God. For years, yea, and ages, Christian? people have been using means for healing, contrary to the teaching of the Bible. Many of these same people would not think of any other way for salvation of the soul except through Jesus, and would say, to climb up any other way would make them thieves and robbers, and yet when it came to healing they never thought of making themselves of the same class by resorting to physicians and medicine.

The true light has once more commenced to shine brilliantly on the earth. The last message is now going forth. The last great conflict is on. In the "evening time it shall be light." The time is now at hand when all Christians will really take up their cross and follow Jesus, no matter how hard the fight. In a short time people will not be considered Christians, even by the world, who resort to medical aid in time of sickness. There are many precious people whose faith is not up to that point yet, but the light is spreading so rapidly, and so many are being healed, that many who are not quite up yet in their faith will, ere long, lay hold of the better way, and feel they are transgressors of God's laws and enemies of the cross of Christ (Phil. 3:18) if they appeal for help in any other way than that which the Bible prescribes.

In His last message to His disciples Jesus gave as one of the signs that would follow the believer that "they shall lay hands on the sick, and they shall recover." Besides this, James gives us explicit directions as to what should be done in case of sickness. "Is any sick among you? let him call for the elders of the church; and let them pray over him, anointing him with oil in the name of the Lord. And the prayer of faith shall save the sick, and the Lord shall raise him up." (James 5:14.)

There is no other plan given in the Bible for healing except through Christ by the wonder-working power of God. Some say they believe in asking God to bless the means or remedies, but their belief is without foundation, for the Bible gives no such directions. People have a good many opinions and practices that are contrary to the teaching of Scripture. The time has now come for Christians to conform completely to the Bible teaching. You can't plead ignorance any longer. Light and knowledge are increasing rapidly as the last message is going forth and the storm clouds are gathering and thickening for the last great conflict.

The Holy Ghost is our teacher. Many, who a year ago could take medicine, would feel condemned, now, to use remedies. The Holy Ghost is constantly testifying of Jesus as Savior, healer and coming King. Homes are being revolutionized. Customs among Christians are changing. The Holy Ghost is at the head and directing these changes. He is seeking those who will honor their Lord and obey Him in everything. He is seeking for a bride for Jesus. When she is fully prepared and has made herself ready and the Lord descends in the air, she, with others, will rise to meet Him, but evidently none will go who are still holding to medicine and remedies.

The atonement is complete, then why not get the complete benefits from it? Why not take the money you have been spending for medicines and physicians and put it in the Lord's work? Healing by the power of God has been advocated by a few for years, but it is now time for the masses of believers in Christ to adopt this standard. Jesus said, "How-

beit when he, the Spirit of truth is come, he will
guide you into all truth;   * * * *   He shall glorify me, for he shall receive of mine, and shall show
it unto you." (John 16:13, 14.)   Healing is a part of
the   truth,   and   He will eventually guide all who
love Jesus into this truth, and this will glorify Him.

In one of his discourses soon after Pentecost, Peter said God was glorifying His Son Jesus in healing
the lame man.   (Acts 3:13.)   When we are healed
by the power of God we glorify Jesus, but otherwise we rather bring a reproach on His name because of our faithlessness; claiming to be Christians
(Christ-like), and then resort to other sources for
healing instead of in the atonement Christ made for
us.

But I wish to repeat, The time is at hand when all
Christians will apply the Bible remedy for sickness
rather than resort to man's remedies.   To fail to do
this means to fall back into disobedience, darkness,
rebellion and sin.   But the outlook is glorious.
Wonderful advances have been made in the last
four years, since the falling of the "latter rain."
The advance will no doubt be more rapid in the
next four years if the Lord tarries.

To accept Christ in these days means to take Him
for Savior, sanctifier, baptizer with the Holy Ghost,
healer and coming King.   He was manifested to
destroy the works of the devil.   (Jno. 3:8.)   Be-

cause of Adam's transgression we are made subject to disease and sickness, but by our obedience and faith in Him Jesus will heal us! "If ye abide in me, and my words abide in you, ye shall ask what ye will, and it shall be done unto you." (Jno. 15:7.) What better promise could we ask than this! Glory! Look up, dear sick one, Jesus is your friend. He will come and heal you if you will ask Him, and submit to His ways.

Oh, just ask Him now to heal you,
   He will never say you, nay!
He has promised to stand by you,
   He's the truth, the life, the way.

CHAPTER X.

THE HOLY GHOST

AND

THE EVIDENCE OF HIS BAPTISM.

We wish to write on this important subject because of a strong tendency almost everywhere among the people to quiet down about it, and because this is one of the main points of criticism by our opposers.

We are not seeking for controversy, but wish to present the facts as they appear in the Holy Scriptures.

We wish to use our influence to draw the minds of the people back to the Bible, and if possible cause more people to press on in the Christian life until they reach the same experience enjoyed by the Holy Apostles and Christians living in their day, because it will require nothing less to accomplish the great and valued task of carrying this gospel of the kingdom into all the world for a witness in obedience to the command of our Savior and Lord.

Jesus gave his disciples special instructions about receiving the Holy Ghost. There are three chapters in St. John's gospel alone largely occupied by this theme. Then if the Lord should take so much time, and John use so much space on this subject it is surely a subject of no little worth, and not to be despised or neglected.

In mentioning the Holy Ghost John refers to Him by using several different names, but explains how that every name he uses refers to the same person.

He is called, "Another Comforter," "The Spirit of truth," "The Holy Ghost," "Holy Spirit," "Spirit of God," "Spirit," etc., all referring to the same person—the third person in the trinity, God, the Father, Jesus Christ the Son, and the Comforter, which is the Holy Ghost. Notice, too, that when the pronoun is used it is masculine gender, showing that He is a real, living person, the same as the Father and the Son. He is not a mere influence, but a real person.

God the Father has proven His ability to talk, by talking face to face with many characters named in the Bible. Adam, Noah, Abraham, Moses and a host of others heard the voice of God the Father.

Jesus Christ the Son has proven His ability to talk as a person by talking to his disciples, the scribes and pharisees and the multitudes.

The Holy Ghost has not fallen short in proving Himself able to do the same thing.

True, God is a spirit, but when talking He not infrequently assumed some sort of body. When talking to Moses He appeared as a "burning bush." On Mount Sinai in fire, thick darkness and a cloud.

Jesus Christ the Son appeared in a human body that walked, ate and talked as we do. It is not out of order or wrong for the Holy Ghost to need a body in which to move and talk. Hence, Paul declares that our bodies are for His use in which He is expected to dwell. "What? know ye not that your body is the temple of the Holy Ghost which is in you, which you have of God, and ye are not your own? For ye are bought with a price: therefore glorify God in your body, and in your spirit, which are God's." (1 Cor. 6:19, 20.) "I beseech you therefore, brethren, by the mercies of God, that ye present your bodies a living sacrifice, holy, acceptable unto God, which is your reasonable service." (Rom. 12:1.)

Then as He is to possess and dwell in human bodies He is not compelled to remain silent any more than the Father and the Son. Jesus gave special information as to what He would do when He came. Jesus said—"He shall glorify me." (John 16:14.) Then whatever He does in and with the human body He possesses and in which He abides is glorifying Jesus, no matter how it looks or what people say or think about it. "He will reprove (convince: margin) the world of sin, and of righteousness, and of judgment." (John 16:8.) In the human body which He possesses he is to do this; then let Him alone, and not criticise His actions and talking. He is both glorifying Jesus and convincing the world of sin, of righteousness, and of judgment.

Jesus tells us, also, that He is a teacher even of all things. "But the Comforter, which is the Holy Ghost, whom the Father will send in my name, He shall teach you all things, and bring all things to your remembrance whatsoever I have said unto you." (John 14:26.) Then if He is to be a teacher and a reminder, could any one object to Him talking in and by the human body he possesses and in which he abides?

A teacher is expected to talk while he is instructing his pupils. He must do this either by words uttered or by signs or writing. The Holy Ghost has a perfect right to use His temple or human body in which He dwells, in talking, making signs or writing. People would not grant Him this privilege if they could help it, but He has it just the same.

Jesus told His disciples how they would know when the Holy Ghost came into their bodies to dwell. He told them plainly that when He came in He would testify of Him (Jesus). "But when the Comforter is come, whom I will send unto you from the Father, even the Spirit of truth which proceedeth from the Father he shall testify of me." (John 15:26.) Now in order for a person to testify he must do it by the use of words, signs or writing. As the Holy Ghost is a person, and not just a mere influence as so many think, He must testify by words signs or writing.   He has a perfect right to testify in words, signs and writing as well as any other person.

The word, SHALL, in the above Scriptural quotation, leaves no room for doubts.   Jesus did not say when He comes He may testify, but makes it positive, and says "He shall testify."   So when He comes into your body, His temple, to abide you may expect Him to testify in words, for He is not dumb, like a god of stone, that He cannot speak. It is, also, probable that He will show some signs by the operations of the body—His temple.   It is not out of place if He should testify in writing by taking the hand or both hands of the body—His temple— and use them by His power.   It remains a fact that when He comes He shall testify.

"He shall not speak of Himself; but whatsoever he shall hear, that shall he speak."   (John 16:13.) Then when He comes He speaks.   This teaching was demonstrated on the day of Pentecost.   Jesus led His disciples out to Bethany and blessed them, and in obedience to His command, they returned to Jerusalem filled with great joy, but they never acknowledged the Holy Ghost had come until the testimony was given by the Spirit Himself.   "And they were all filled with the Holy Ghost, and began to speak with other tongues, as the Spirit gave them utterance."   (Acts 2:4.)   There were also signs given in some kind of operations of the body, for these disciples were accused of being drunk, which indicates some form of demonstration.

The same truth is demonstrated in the tenth chapter of Acts, where the Spirit fell upon the household of Cornelius. "And they of the circumcision which believed were astonished, as many as came with Peter, because that on the Gentiles also was poured out the gift of the Holy Ghost. For they heard them speak with tongues and magnify God." (Acts 10:45, 46.) Then Peter acknowledged that they had received the Holy Ghost as well as those who were in the upper room at Jerusalem, which evidently he would not have done if he had not heard them speak with tongues as the Spirit gave utterance. Peter emphasized this thought when he said, "The Holy Ghost fell on them, as on us at the beginning. Then remembered I the word of the Lord, how that he said, John indeed baptized with water; but ye shall be baptized with the Holy Ghost. Forasmuch then as God gave them the like gift as he did unto us, who believed on the Lord Jesus Christ; what was I, that I could withstand God?" (Acts 11:15-17.)

How did Peter and the Jews who were with him know the Gentiles had received the Holy Ghost? Let the Bible answer. "For they heard them speak with tongues." (Acts 10:46.) And Peter could also have said just as truthfully that he remembered the words of the Lord when He said, when the Holy Ghost comes to an individual to abide He will testify. This same truth is illustrated at Acts 19:6. "And when Paul had laid his hands upon them, the Holy Ghost came on them; and they spake with tongues, and prophesied."

Then with all these Scriptures as proof we are on solid footing when we say that speaking in tongues as the Spirit gives utterance is the evidence of the baptism with the Holy Ghost. And if that evidence was needed for Jesus' disciples and the mother of our Lord, the same unmistakable evidence is needed to-day. There has never been any change made in the teaching of Scripture; the only change that has ever been made about speaking in other tongues as the Spirit gives utterance being the evidence of tne baptism with the Holy Ghost, has been made by false teachers.

We are not giving our opinion about this matter we are giving the infallible Word of God for it. We do not shrink from saying that when people teach otherwise they make themselves false teachers, and fulfill the Scriptures at 2 Peter 2:1, 2. "But there were false prophets also among the people, even as there shall be false teachers among you, who privily shall bring in damnable heresies, even denying the Lord that bought them, and bring upon themselves

swift destruction.   And many shall follow their per-
nicious ways; by reason of whom the way of truth
shall be evil spoken of."

In writing upon this subject we would not feel it
necessary to make it so emphatic and radical were
it not for the opposition shown by so many profes-
sors of the Christian religion to this sacred and all
important truth.   Then, too, we are living in a time
when truth must be brought to light and a decided
and uncompromising stand taken for it, the same as
the Holy Apostles stood for it in the beginning of
the gospel dispensation.

God is now raising up a people to engage in this
last great struggle and conflict against formalism,
perverted Scriptures and theories of men, who will
sacrifice their lives, if need be, rather than surrender any part of the truth that came from the sacred
lips of Jesus, and the inspired pens of the Apostles.
After a careful and prayerful searching and study,
for more than four years, we are sure we are on a
solid foundation when we say that no one has ever
been baptized with the Holy Ghost without speaking
with other tongues as the Spirit gave them utterance.
We admit that this teaching is opposed by many
writers and teachers, but no opposition of men and
the combined forces of hell can succeed in eradi-
cating this precious truth from the Bible.

This blessed old Book has stood the tests of ages

and has been opposed in every generation since its origin, but to-day it has a wider circulation than any time in the history of the past. If the Bible could be destroyed then we would have nothing to depend upon that is infallible; but the experience of thousands in our day, even then, is a fact that would not be easily stamped out of existence in two or three future generations.

This "Latter Rain" movement is characterized by certain signs which distinguish it from all so-called pentecostal movements on the earth to-day; and these signs have drawn the fire of the enemy from every quarter, and brought down storms of criticism. Those who are too weak to stand the fire in the conflict with the enemy, not willing to be made targets, have compromised those truths and demonstrations which draw the fire.

Satan knows that the speaking in tongues as at Pentecost, Acts 2:4, and at the house of Cornelius, Acts 10:46, and at Ephesus, Acts 19:6, is the evidence that a person is baptized with the Holy Ghost, and this being the case, he is bringing all his power to bear and uniting his forces against this one point.

As so many have weakened on the doctrine and compromised on the blessed truth of God, especially as to the tongues being the evidence of the baptism with the Holy Ghost, and are trying to do away with all manifestations and demonstrations of the Spirit, we feel under renewed obligations, moved by the Spirit of God, to rush into the conflict and raise our voice to a higher pitch and move our pen with more alacrity and dexterity to hold up the full standard of pentecost in every particular phase.

We are not of those who are drawing back, but we are pressing forward toward the deeper and greater things, where greater and more sensational wonders will be brought forth from obscurity, so it may be said of us as at Pentecost, "He hath shed forth this which ye now see and hear." (Acts 2:33.) "For the promise is unto you, and to your children, and to all that are afar off, even as many as the Lord our God shall call." (Acts 2:39.)

CHAPTER XI.

The Spirit was poured out on the one hundred and twenty on the day of Pentecost, which set in motion God's great machine that was to continue in operation until certain things were accomplished.

There was such a stupendous outpouring that the results from it startled the whole city of Jerusalem. "Now when this was noised abroad, the multitude came together, and were confounded." The effect was of great magnitude, even to the extreme. Three thousand souls were added to their ranks in one day.

Another thing worthy of our attention at this point is the fact that "they continued steadfastly in the apostle's doctrine and fellowship."

Then immediately following this great ingathering of souls, (and some believe it to have been the same day), there was another great ingathering, which surpassed that of the first, and this time reached the enormous sum of five thousand men, and very likely as many or more women and children.

The inference is that as they were added to the first company of one hundred and twenty, and the additional three thousand, that this vast multitude continued steadfastly in the Apostle's doctrine and fellowship; making in all probably about thirteen thousand one hundred and twenty, all in fellowship and the one doctrine.

No matter what had been their views and opinions of the past, all these vanished at once under the mighty blaze of Pentecostal glory and power They were so completely changed by the white heat and wonderful transforming power of God that they knew only one doctrine, and therefore they were in full fellowship. One in Spirit and one in doctrine.

There is one other experience or manifestation that should not be left unnoticed. "And there appeared unto them cloven tongues like as of fire, and it sat upon each of them." (Acts 2:3.) This now gives us three particular points specially noticeable and of vast importance in connection with the discussion of our subject. To these three we add one more, and then together with the speaking in tongues as the Spirit gives utterance, the signs, wonders miracles, healings, etc., and we get back to Pentecost. This fourth and last point is the spread of the gospel in all the world during the life-time of those first baptized with the Holy Ghost.

The commission given them to "be witnesses unto me both in Jerusalem, and in all Judea, and in Samaria, and unto the uttermost part of the earth," was accomplished in that generation. "Their sound went into all the earth, and their words unto the ends of the world." (Rom. 10:18.) "Which was preached to every creature which is under heaven." (Col. 1:23.)

Here, then, are the four points that should not be neglected or overlooked, and are evidently essential to Pentecost: "Cloven tongues like as of fire, and it sat upon each of them;" the multitudes of God's children to continue steadfastly in the Apostle's doctrine and fellowship; the great ingathering of souls; and the spread of the gospel into all the world in the generation in which they lived, upon whom was poured out the gift of the Holy Ghost.

In the light of these Scriptures, then we are some distance from the fullness of Pentecost, even though we are sure of the infilling and indwelling of the Holy Spirit. We really have the evidence of the baptism with the Holy Ghost, and there is no doubt of that part of Pentecost, but we must admit that the conversion of three thousand and five thousand under one sermon by a Peter is lacking yet. Also, we have not attained to unity in doctrine, neither are we perfect yet in fellowship. And as to the spread of this glorious gospel to the ends of the world, to say the least about it, we have a service before us of great magnitude.

The people are settling down content without the cloven tongues like as of fire sitting upon each of them. Multitudes of them are declaring that we

can never reach the unity or oneness of doctrine, and thus are making no efforts to teach unity
or bring it about. Still others are glorying over a
revival where twenty or thirty are converted in a
two or three weeks meeting, and perfectly content
without reaching forth and contending for the three
or five thousand under one sermon.

There may be a very few who have the interest
of souls, and the spread of our Lord's gospel into
all the world in this generation, so on their hearts
that they are groaning and crying and giving the
Lord no rest till they get back to Pentecost with all
it means, but do we have any who are willing and
able to make the sacrifice and ventures that it will
take to reach the fullness of Pentecost?

Many are losing out and going back entirely. Why
is this? Simply because they must either go on to
greater heights and attainments in the Christian life
or go back. To go forward the price is too high to
pay; the cross too heavy to bear. They fall back
to an easier way, that carries with it no reproach or
persecutions. They lose their power because they
are afraid to venture forward. God is demanding
something more of them, and they halt. Thoughts
of fanaticism and what people will say stare them
in the face. Their first love and fervency fades
away, and they soon fall back into their former rank,
and are lost to view from Pentecostal circles. Once

looked upon as leaders, but will soon be forgotten, and their places will be filled with others whom God can trust.

Beloved, we are facing a stupendous problem. The last issue of the age. It is the last great conflict. It is either go back to Pentecost in its fullness, which means all we have outlined above, or fade as a leaf, and wither and finally lose our hold on the vine (Jesus), and be blown away by the first wind of autumn, or the first wind of the great storm of tribulation that will soon burst forth with tremendous fury upon this generation of idolatry, pleasure and wickedness.

We have something more to do. We must nerve ourselves up on every line. The tensions must be tightened .to the very highest pitch, ready for the conflict with the already furious foe, for his satanic majesty knows his time is short, and will invent every wily scheme that in his wisdom will prove advantageous for his hellish purpose. We dare not go into camp here. We must be on the open battle field. The fullness of Pentecost is just ahead.

The promised land was just ahead of Israel when they landed at Kadeshbarnea, but they said there were giants over there and they were not able to overcome them. Cities whose walls reached up to the sky. "We cannot go over and possess the land," they said. They lingered all night long. Trouble in the camp while they delayed going over, but they did not move on. They waited a few hours too long; until God said they could not go. Then they presumed to go up, but it was a failure.

Look out, beloved, we may linger here on the border land one day or an hour too long and be put to shame, and thus lose the better things that are promised us, and the incoming generation gain the land we might have enjoyed, if we had only pressed over at the proper time.

The fullness of Pentecost. Who will be a Caleb and still the people and say to them, We are fully able, let us go up at once and possess the land. Who will listen at, and obey the voice of our Captain and press on until you are filled with all the fullness of God? You dare not tarry on the threshold; you must either push on inside or be roughly thrust backward. But the people are satisfied without the "tongues like as of fire" sitting on each of them. They are satisfied and contented without the unity of faith and one doctrine for all. They are satisfied without the three and five thousand converts under one sermon. Satisfied without this gospel going to all the world for a witness in our day. The undertaking is too great. They love home too well. They love the family tie too well to break it. "It is a shame," they say, "to leave our wives and children, our homes and friends, and venture out on the promises of God for support."

We venture to say that there will be, and is now, a Caleb and a Joshua that will not rest, neither give others rest, until they have obtained the fullness of Pentecost with all it means. We have started to go through, and God helping us we must get back to Pentecost in its fullness. Who will join our ranks and contend for the faith once delivered to the saints, and pray for the tongues like as of fire, to rest upon each of you?

Who will fall in with the Apostle's doctrine, and get rid of all false notions, theories and opinions with which you may have been filled? Who will join with us in contending for the conversion of three and five thousand souls under one sermon, with a powerful and fiery church in prayer while the preacher stands before the multitudes and delivers the message freighted with the power from heaven.

Who will make the sacrifice and go forth to conquer or die on the field to get this gospel of the kingdom to every creature under heaven in this generation? Will you? Will you? Is the responsibility too great? Is the cross too heavy to bear? Is home and friends too dear and comfortable for you to make the sacrifice? Will God let you take an easier place nearer home, and give you as great rewards? Do you want to content yourself and be satisfied with anything short of the fullness of Pentecost? You can remain in the back ground if you wish, but rest assured that God will find some one who will burst through all opposition, disabuse his mind of false teaching and theology, and step off before you and win the laurels in the conflict, while you are standing back all bewildered and your mind beclouded with doubts and fears, wondering what has caused such a sensation, until it will be too late for you to even pick up the spoils after the smoke has cleared away from the bloody battle field.

Saul and his army of trained soldiers were held back by the bold challenge of Goliath, the Philistine giant, when David, who had never seen a battle, except his battle with the lion and bear, hastily picked up the five stones and put them in his shepherd's bag and rushed off to meet him who had defied all Israel. While the astonished king and his soldiers looked on with amazement little David was severing the head of the giant from his shoulders with his own sword, and running back triumphantly carrying the head of the enemy.

Hundreds of trained missionaries are on the field to-day, but soon a few little Davids who have gotten back to Pentecost will burst on the scene, fly past them all and win the great battle and evangelize the world, while those who have been toiling so long will be looking on with amazement and wonder.

CHAPTER XII.

THE FULLNESS OF PENTECOST.

There are none so hungry for the demonstration of God's great power as those who are nearest to it. From many quarters comes the cry, from Spirit filled souls, for the manifestations of God's power as was shown in the time of the Apostles.

From the fact that this hunger and desire is created in God's children proves that He who creates such desires is also desirous to bestow it, and will do so when proper conditions are met.

We are evidently entering the penumbra, and soon will break out the full wave, and the signs of an Apostle will be seen in hundreds, yea thousands of God's children as they run to and fro all over the world.

We now have great sympathy for the lame, halt and blind, deaf, dumb and sick; but so far have been unable to relieve suffering humanity only to a limited extent. Whilst it is true many have been miraculously healed, yet with all that has been done we are limited in reaching the masses. Far reaching, sensational results and instances have been very rare.

I do not say this to discourage, but rather mean it to encourage us to press on and not be satisfied to rest where we are. We can't "hold our own" long,

for if we don't go forward we will soon find ourselves slipping back down the slope, not having
reached the goal.

Some people may think we are putting too much
stress on the church and her glory and power, but
we are in the battle to win, and there is no retreat
to be tolerated. I can bear with others who seem
to grow cold and weary in the race, who show less
fervency and zeal than when they first entered the
experience of the baptism with the Holy Ghost, but
I cannot bear such cooling off in myself.

I have received some letters of warning and criticism, and I wish to show respect to all, the best I
can, but there is no compromise allowed. It is my
purpose to agitate this question until the results are
seen—the church fully established with all of her
former glory and power, gifts and graces. We must
not be content to allow the work to go on even as it
is. Encouraging reports are coming in from many
places; we hear of good results, but we must not let
the good things keep us from obtaining the best.
The Spirit has said many times, "You are too slow
—too fearful." Jesus told the disciples they were
slow of heart to believe. We must hurry on, and
dare not stop here.

Ere long, some who are prominent now will be
lost to view. No doubt people will wonder what
has become of them. They will be wanted in camp

meetings—in other meetings, but they cannot be found. Mail will not reach them. Their families may not even know their whereabouts; no one will know but God. Elijah was down at the brook alone many days. The ravens fed him, and there he remained until he received orders. He finally wandered to a perishing widow's home, raised her dead son to life, and then all of a sudden burst forth from seclusion and showed himself to king Ahab, who was his enemy. Soon the fire fell on the sacrifice in the presence of a mocking, idolatrous crowd, four hundred of the prophets of Baal were slain by this mighty man of God, then the rain came down in torrents in answer to his prayer. This all came to pass after he had been hidden away with God alone for a long time.

Little groups will be formed to pray for the power and gifts of the Spirit. Individuals will be lost to this world, with their faces buried in their hands as they lay prostrate on the ground before God. Listen at them as they pray, with tears streaming down from their eyes and their voices trembling with emotion and the power of God. "Lord, I must have the power as it was given the Apostles or I can go no further. I am not able to preach another sermon or conduct another meeting in the common way, I must have some special help from Thee." Then a fresh flow of tears, and only a

groan will be uttered at intervals as they tarry.
Night will come on, but unnoticed by the earnest
seeker. No desire for food. No care for prominence. No desire for leadership. No greed for
money. No care for this world and its pleasures or
business interests. They are only thirsting after
God. They want Him. They are toiling to get in
connection with God's great magazine of power.
They would rather die than fail to get it and live.
As John Knox cried out as he lay in an agony of
prayer all night long, "Give me Scotland or give me
death!" so if you could steal upon those groups of
prayers, or slip out where one is praying alone, you
would probably hear him say, "Give me this power
or give me death!"

All reformations have been strewed more or less
with tears, groans and earnest, soul stirring, agonizing prayers. This is the greatest one yet, so we
shall expect no less suffering, agonizing prayers and
groans; in fact this is to be, and is the greatest and
final consummation that will not only effect and stir
a few nations, but the world will not only feel it, but
will be involved and evangelized. The saints will
be caught away, the tribulation will burst forth and
do its deadly work, and Jesus with His great army
will ride down from heaven and subdue all things
to Himself. The devil will be chained, the beast
and false prophet thrown alive into the lake of fire,

and Jesus and His saints take complete control of this world.

All this just ahead, yea, so near, and we, His children, grow careless and cold, lose energy, zeal and courage at such a time as this? No! No! Oh, No!! All this almost on us and His children, like spoiled babies fussing over toys, back-biting, criticising each other, caviling over opinions and petty notions, carrying tales and talking about one another in a way to wound and hurt feelings, will not repent, neither will they forgive and look over faults and mistakes of the past, but continue to hold grudges, malice, envy, etc.? Oh, surely not! Time is too precious to use it in any such a way.

We have time for but one thing now. To go on as we have been is futile. To stop is dangerous. To go back means eternal damnation. Beloved, we must press on and reach the original in all of its phases. We have teachers (too many, for some are false teachers), pastors, evangelists, and prophets to a slight degree, but no Apostles are known yet. There is no doubt there are men living who will develop into Apostles, but no one can palm himself off on us as an Apostle who is not, for the unmistakable signs will prove him the same as the sign of tongues proves the baptism with the Holy Ghost.

Tongues evidences the baptism as on the day of Pentecost, but there are as truly signs that will evidence and single out the Apostles until they cannot be hidden, when they are fully developed. That lame man hobbling down the street yonder, see him as he limps! He must be made to walk! A few words from an Apostle, and a touch of the hand, and the old cane or crutch will be thrown aside, and the poor cripple leaping and shouting at the top of his voice, until all the folks on Main street will begin to think a lunatic has escaped from the asylum.

See that poor, pitiful looking man, all humped up and drawn together, yonder in that wheel chair. What is the matter with him? Rheumatism. Incurable! Send for Peter (an apostle), let him walk beside the chair, and his shadow fall on the poor helpless invalid. All of a sudden a cry of astonishment is heard. The chair is suddenly vacated. What has happened? Only an Apostle passed by, that's all. But the whole country hears of it. Where is the Apostle? He is gone to the city of G———. Go down to the railroad station, watch every train as they come in. Help! Help! The train men are unable to handle the cripples, so they call for help. Where is he (the Apostle)? The cripples are all placed on the platform, and very soon the Apostle passes along and touches every one, and all are healed, and running and shouting until the whole city comes together and demands an explanation. Now is the opportunity. The multitudes have gathered.

Upon an old goods box or an express wagon he stands to explain, when after a few words about Jesus and faith in His name, and God glorifying His Son Jesus, three, five, yea ten thousand people will surrender and accept such a Christ as that. Hallelujah!

But wait a moment! Hear! Listen! Oh, it's only a blind man! But see, he gropes his way along all in utter darkness,has not seen the light of the sun, the green vegetation, the beautiful structures, nor the faces of loved ones for years. What a pitiable sight! You must have a heart of stone if you do not pity him.. The humble, loving, sympathetic Apostle comes near, and suddenly, like a flash, a stream of light appears, and those once faded, sunken eyes sparkle with delight as they once more behold the faces of friends and the beauty of nature. Noised abroad? Oh yes, and all will be healed! Glory! The sick, the deaf, the dumb, all will be healed, every one. (Acts 5:12-16.)

But stay! Why that weeping and screaming and people rushing in and about that house yonder? What has happened? A woman has just died, and she was the only support of an aged widowed mother. Send for Peter (the Apostle). He sees the situation. Nothing is especially strange; many have died. In fact, death is only a gateway to heaven to those who are prepared. But wait a moment, let us see what he will do. Lovingly, tenderly, gently, he puts them all out of the room and fastens the door. There he is alone with a corpse. Look in at the keyhole in the door. He kneels down and prays; then turns suddenly and takes the corpse by the hand, and says, "Tabitha, arise." (Acts 9:40.) Has anything happened? Suddenly the door is opened, and there stands she that was dead in the bloom of youth and a picture of health.

No good in that, you say? Yes, but the whole city will be stirred. (Acts 9:42.) The newspapers and telephones and telegraphs' will herald the miracle far and wide, and thousands will believe and say good by to old forms and creeds, and will be stanch followers of Christ. (Acts 9:35.)

How rapidly the world will be evangelized with such as that as a daily occurrence in every country and on every island of the sea! The lame ought to walk, the sick ought to be healed, the blind ought to see, the deaf ought to hear, the dumb ought to speak, the dead ought to be raised to life again, the poor ought to have the gospel preached to them. Yes, all this is for us, and just ahead, and who would dare faint by the way?

"Power to heal the leper,
Power to raise the dead,
Power to fill the empty pots with oil;
Is waiting for the worker,
Who in Jesus' steps will tread,
And leave this life of ease for one of toil."

CHAPTER XIII.

THE BRIDE. CHURCH, BODY. KINGDOM
AND
FAMILY OR HOUSEHOLD OF GOD.

As there has been so much written on the above subjects, and so many different opinions expressed, I'm sure no one can offer any legal objections if I should write a few thoughts and give a few Scriptural references bearing on the same.

Some teach that when we are converted we then become members of the Kingdom, and some that we are born into the church, while others teach that when we are baptized with the Holy Ghost we are members of the bride.

The latest teaching that has come to my notice, from the pen of a noted writer in a Pentecostal paper, is that we are baptized (by the Holy Ghost) into the church, and that the church is the bride. The same writer teaches that people are born into the kingdom and baptized into the church by the Spirit, and that the bride, the church, and the body are all one and the same, and the terms are used interchangeably.

These are all interesting themes, and worthy of consideration, but to give an exhaustive discussion on each one separate would require more space than can be allotted at this time. And to fully understand these subjecs is not so important any way as to have a real and full experience of salvation and know it.

While there are various opinions expressed by word and pen regarding these terms and their relation to each other, yet the facts remain the same and no strain can possibly produce any variation.

If people are born into the church, then Jude was mistaken about certain men CREEPING in whom he said were ungodly men (Jude 4), and Paul when he declared false brethren were BROUGHT in (Gal. 2:4). If people are born into the church Paul was certainly mistaken again when he gave orders to the church at Corinth to gather themselves together and put away from among themselves that wicked person. (1 Cor. 5:4, 13.) If they are born into the church they will have to become unborn to get out of it, and the members of the church themselves will have no more to do with putting them out than taking them in. Such teaching is erroneous and inconsistent, and contrary to the teachings of Scripture.

The same writer that unhesitatingly declares it is wrong to teach that we are born into the church, teaches that we are baptized into the church when we receive the baptism with the Holy Ghost. By such teaching the writer asserts that no person can be a member of Christ's church without having the baptism with the Holy Ghost, and gives as a proof text 1 Cor. 12:13, and says—"born into the kingdom. baptized into the body " the church.

If this teaching is correct then Paul was wrong when he wrote "Unto the church of God which is at Corinth," and in the first verse of chapter three said: "And I, brethren, could not speak unto you as unto spiritual, but as unto carnal, even as unto babes in Christ," and follows by saying in the third verse, "For ye are yet carnal." These were in the church of God, and had not yet received the baptism with the Holy Ghost to put them into the church. Facts are very stubborn, people's teachings do not change the blessed old Book.

The same writer affirms that the church is the bride and the bride is the church. If this is true, then the church now must be something different from what it was in John's day, or else a backslidden preacher or pastor has the power to divorce and cast out of the bride one who is espoused to the King, for at 3 John 9 and 10 we read, "I wrote unto the church: but Diotrephes, * * * * casteth them out of the church." If the church and the bride are one and the same then it would do to have it read thus—Diotrephes casteth them out of the bride.

Honest, sincere and humble people can readily

see the inconsistency of such teaching. This is a time when mere theories and false teachings are going to be exposed and the false teachers themselves put out of the ring. Honest, sincere men and women are studying for themselves now as never before.

We are truly living in "perilous times," and a time when it is a matter of the greatest importance to be humble and sincere before God, for we are liable to be misguided and lose our rewards, if not our souls. It is no wonder that Peter wrote thus: "Wherefore, beloved, seeing that ye look for such things, be diligent that ye may be found of him in peace, without spot and blameless. And account that the long suffering of our Lord is salvation; even as our beloved brother Paul also according to the wisdom given unto him hath written unto you; as also in all his epistles, speaking in them of these things; in which are some things hard to be understood, which they that are unlearned and unstable wrest, as they do also the other scriptures to their own destruction. Ye therefore, beloved, seeing ye know these things before, beware lest ye also, being led away with the error of the wicked, fall from your own steadfastness." (2 Peter 3:14-17.)

This warning given by Peter should be carefully considered and heeded in dealing with the theme now before us. Truly Paul has written things hard to be understood, and he himslf says: "The natural man receiveth not the things of the Spirit of God: for they are foolishness unto him: neither can he know them, because they are spiritually discerned." (1 Cor. 2:14.)

It is not my purpose to merely be a critic, although it is possible to know that some things are wrong, and yet not be able to make them right. A certain man had a watch, which would not keep time. One watch maker after another examined it, pronounced it perfect, but none of them could make it run correctly, and none of them could tell why; until one cunning watch maker counted every cog on every wheel, and found that one wheel had one cog less than the proper number. Although we might see that there is something wrong with the watch, but how few will take the time and trouble to count every cog in every wheel of the watch. We can see that many teachings given by men are erroneous, but how few people will take the time and trouble to count every cog in every wheel that regulates Scripture so it will run correctly.

The terms at the head of this chapter are in God's great plan for the redemption of man and his eternal glory, as the wheels are to the watch. One cog less than the proper number, just in one wheel, made the watch of no value. Paul and Peter, John and Jude have made no mistakes, but how few who

claim to be teachers will take time to consult each
writer on a subject before venturing some kind of
an opinion. It is of the utmost importance that we
who are to be teachers should count every cog in
every wheel before venturing to give out teaching,
lest we sometime find ourselves perverting Scripture.

It is a fact, and people had just as well acknowledge it, for it will be proven sooner or later, that the
true Bible church has been so covered and hidden
with the debris of creeds and theology, that not
until they count every cog in every wheel are they
able to know what the church of God really is, to
say nothing about the bride, which is to be even
more perfect than the church.

You will notice that I have now intimated that
the church and bride are not the same. I will now
call your attention to a few facts that you will observe as such very readily. The bride is one. The
church is one. The kingdom is one. The family or
household is one. God the Father is one. God the
Son is one. God the Holy Ghost is one. Every
wheel in the watch is one wheel. When the wheels
are all geared together properly, and the main-spring
and hair-spring properly adjusted and in the case
wound up, we call it a watch that is running and
marking time.

God the Father, God the Son and God the Holy

Ghost, has each His function to perform, but these three are one. The bride, the church, the body, the kingdom and the family or household of God, each have their place to fill in God's great and eternal plan, and this plan is one plan. As all the wheels and parts are in the watch, and each part performs its function, so all these elements are in God's plan, and each to perform its function. These terms, the bride, the church, the kingdom, etc., are so geared together and have such a close resemblance that unless one takes the time and pains to count the cogs in every one and know its exact position in God's great plan, he is liable to put one for the other and the other for that one.

The human body is one great machine, but it is composed of skin, bones, hair, arteries, veins, muscles, blood, flesh, etc., but it is one great system and body made by God Himself. Anatomists have been able to dissect and locate and name every particle of the human body, but no one person ever discovered and named every particle at his first investigation, neither did one person ever complete the task as it is given in physiology to-day.

People have been investigating the terms of our theme and placing their opinions on them for years, but it is now high time for them to sit down and count every cog in every wheel or give up the job and quit guessing at it. Paul tells us of a people

that will appear in the last days, who will have a
form of godliness, but deny the power, ever learn-
ing, but never able to come to the knowledge of the
truth. (2 Tim. 3:5-7.) But the Holy Spirit is given,
says John, to guide into all truth. (John 14:26 and
John 16:13.) As these are the days of the outpouring of the Holy Ghost, then it is time to quit guessing about things and really count every cog in every
wheel, lest we find ourselves perverting Scripture
and wresting it to our own destruction.

The bride is clearly set forth in Scripture, and she
is beautiful to behold with her loveliness, beauty and
adornment; but Rebecca, who was a type, did not
know that she was to be the bride of Isaac while
she was doing the very things that Abraham's servant prayed that the bride should do. But after she
had really met the requirements without trying to
be the bride, the jewelry was placed upon her.
She did not yet know what it meant, until at the
proper time, when the servant saw she would do,
and that she measured up to every requirement with
perfect ease on her part, because the very nature of
the requirement was in her. The servant then delivered his secret, not only to her, but to her family
as well. The whole family was not chosen, but
they were consulted. The final settlement, however, was made by her as she said, "I will go."

"Hearken, O, daughter, and consider, and incline

thine ear; forget also thine own people, and thy
father's house." (Ps. 45:10.) Here is one little
glimpse of the bride. "Upon thy right hand did
stand the queen in gold of Ophir." Another glimpse.
"She shall be brought unto the king in raiment of
needle work." Look on her in her beautiful array.
"My dove, my undefiled is but one; she is the only
one of her mother, she is the choice one of her
that bear her." (Solomon's Song 6:9.) You get
a picture of her here, but you must count the cogs
or your watch will not keep time. It would make
this chapter too long to produce every Scripture, and
only a glimpse can be given.

While the bride is in such a state of perfection,
look at the church of God at Corinth with members
in it who were not even sanctified; but of course
these were expected to press on to a higher standard
of perfection. Look, too, at those in the churches
of Galatia who were fallen from grace. And see
"The virgins her companions that follow her shall
be brought unto thee. With gladness and rejoicing
shall they be brought: they shall enter into the king's
palace." (Ps. 45:14, 15.) But notice, while they
enter the king's palace they are not the bride. The
wise virgins of Math. 25 are not a part of the bride,
but they have the blessed privilege of entering with
the bride, because of having oil in their vessels with
their lamps. The foolish virgins are virgins, but will

not get in with the others; and yet it is evident they are members of the church, as they seemed to have fellowship with those that did get in.   The wise virgins who are fortunate enough to enter with the bride are evidently members of the church, but not the bridehood saints.

I have not completed the subject, neither have I discussed the body, the kingdom nor the family or household of God, but I have given enough to put you to studying and carefully counting the cogs on the wheels so you will not be mystified or led into error by false teaching you may read or hear.   I hope to be able at some future time to furnish a more complete discussion of each of these great subjects, and their relation to each other and their place in God's great plan.

CHAPTER XIV

THE CHURCH OF GOD.

There is a growing tendency in the minds of the Christian people of to-day to be more favorably impressed with the Church of God.

There is at work an undercurrent, unobserved by the masses, like the electrical current on the wire, which, when properly constructed, connected and utilized, will enable people to understand one another who have been far apart in their teachings of the Bible. The Spirit is doing His work, and is working where we might least expect.

Not a few are looking for the real Bible church to make her appearance who have never heard of the "Church of God" as some of us know her. In the atmosphere seems to be floating an influence that is preparing and moving people unconsciously in the same direction. Sectarian prejudices are crumbling and vanishing under this mighty influence until unions are being effected and plans constructed for enormous religious combinations. But few, and probably none of these instigators know of the undercurrent or influence that is at work, neither do they understand the purport of such actions, but it is God wielding his mighty sceptre preparing the people for the Bible church—the Church of God.

The unrest, the dissatisfaction, the low murmuring, and in many instances the unexpressed feelings
that lie buried beneath the vaults of expression, all
tell the story of the fulfillment of prophecy that the
wise, spoken of by Daniel, can understand.   There
is a deep hunger and longing in the heart of every
child of God, whether known or unknown, that
nothing will ever satisfy but the revelation of the
Bible church and the unity and oneness of God's
people.   To this end is the Spirit working.   To this
end is the unobserved undercurrent making tremendous strides.   No matter about present day appear-
ances or how much this very article or teaching may
be opposed, He will bring it to pass.

Jesus was laid in the tomb and the stone was laid
on the mouth and sealed, and a guard placed around
it, and the appearance was anything else than for
Him to come forth and live; but He came forth with
the same body, bearing the very same scars and
marks that He had when taken down from the cross
and placed therein.   He that brought again from the
dead our Lord Jesus is able, and will bring back
again the original Church, bearing the very same
scars (persecutions,) and marks (signs), that she had
when taken down from her promontory soon after
the last Apostle surrendered his life for her.

The church is the body of Christ (Col. I;24,) then
no surprise if she follow her Lord into obscurity

and then make her appearance again. Jesus appeared to Mary, then to Peter and the two as they walked to Emmaus, then to the eleven as they sat at meat, and finally to five hundred brethren at one time. The church is now appearing to a few, but some of these are like the disciples, who at one time did not know Jesus, they do not know the church. Not a few are now confusing her with other churches, but she is not like other churches in many respects.

We have been grieved at times when we have known of some of the members having the common church principles so imbibed in their natures that they expect and urge the same to be effective in the Church of God. The rules and plans used in the common churches of the day would unbalance and deface the Church of God. Our officers and members should act very cautious, and seek for and use great wisdom, lest her visage should be marred and she "wounded in the house of her friends."

The overseers, bishops, deacons and entire membership should not pattern after the same order in other churches, but should seek for wisdom and instruction from God and His Word as to duties and responsibilities. There is a tendency in the human, when placed in honored positions, to feel and act their importance. This is commonly known or expressed as dignity. There is and should be in every child of God a degree of real true dignity, but not a whitewashed or selfish so-called dignity.

The church with its combination of humility, meekness, splendor and glory is observed by only a few at present, but soon she will be revealed to thousands. Hallelujah! At this present time she is ranked alongside with other churches in the minds of many, and from a lack of knowing her perfectly by some of the members themselves, is sometimes a cause for some little friction and division; but as the members become more acquainted with her and her laws and rules, these disturbances will vanish from sight.

Men who have been accustomed to dictating in other churches, or under the rules of other churches, expect the same course to be pursued in the Church of God, and all these imperfections hinder the progress and bestowment of God's power to an extent, but when she assumes perfect order and is free from the opinions and dictatorial tendencies of man great things will be accomplished.

Notice that picture of the original Church as outlined in the Acts of the Apostles and placed in a nutshell in Solomon's Song 6:10. "Who is she that looketh forth as the morning, fair as the moon, clear as the sun, and terrible as an army with banners." Did not the Church, fresh from the hands of Him who said, "Upon this rock I'll build my church,"

look forth in the morning of the gospel age? Was
she not as fair as the moon shining forth her light
and soft silvery rays into the darkness of the time?
Wasn't her light borrowed from Jesus Christ her
head, as the moon borrows her light from that great
luminary called the sun? Did she not burst forth as
the sun, sending out both light and heat (knowledge
and power), until it could be said of her that she
was "clear as the sun," until she was seen by all
who were not wilfully blind, and did not even they
feel her searching rays of influence?

With all the miracles, manifestations of power,
her wonderful increase daily and rapid progress until
it was said, "These that turn the world upside down
hath come hither also," could it not be well said of
her, "And terrible as an army with banners?"

Then, as if the winter blasts had come, and the
fervency had been chilled by the coldness and
blackness of the "dark ages," and the body (the
Church) lying silent in the tomb, the seer, apparently with a hope of seeing some signs of life
and a resurrection of the body (the Church) says,
"I went down into the garden of nuts to see the fruits
of the valley, and to see whether the vine flourished,
and the pomegranates budded." (Cant. 6:11.) As
he was in active seeking for the signs of life, or a
search after truth, all of a sudden, as though by
magic, light dawned, and the seer could see, like the

passing of a panorama before him, the outline of what was to come to pass, and burst forth with an exclamation of mingled surprise and joy expressed in Can. 6:12. "Or ever I was aware, my soul made me like the chariots of Aminadib," and he was brought to his senses, and suddenly a sense of high aspiration seized hold of him as he cried out, "Return, return, O Shulamite; return, return, that we may look upon thee." Then, as if in comparison with the conditions illustrated in the tenth verse as she first sprang into view, in answer to the question "What will ye see in the Shulamite?" remarked with deep thought and magnified prospects, "As It were the company of two armies."

The explanation is apparent, the comparison is clear. The cry is now by thousands of lovers of truth for the return of the early Apostolic Church with all her former glory, power and results. Searchers after truth in the valley of humiliation have suddenly been encouraged and amazed as the Spirit and Scriptures have revealed to them the fact that she is going to return with all her gifts and graces, power and glory, and instead of being as she was at the first, in respect to magnitude and sublimity she will be double. "As it were the company of two armies." Hallelujah! Hallelujah! rings out from the vortex of emotional, jubilant, triumphal expression in every lover of God as they comprehend and behold even a shadow of this glorious glaring truth.

The cries and groans for Apostolic methods, practices and glory will be realized in the near future. There has been a slight lull, and many have grown a little cold and lost a little in zeal and courage, but listen—there is a sound of an abundance of rain. The church that is already in existence is now being refreshed. The members are now receiving a new impetus. The Seventh Annual Assembly was wonderful. More light is showing, and revealing hidden treasures every year. Man's ways and plans are fading from view. God's ways and plans are being revealed.

Soon will be heard the startling sound of tramp, tramp, tramp, as the "Company of two armies" go marching through the land into every city, town, plain and jungle, heralding the last message: "Fear God and give glory to Him (Rev. 15:6, 7), until this gospel of the kingdom is preached in all the world."

The budding time has come and is almost over; soon, and very soon, will the flowers of Pentecost burst wide open and radiate their fragrant perfume into the nostrils of the lovers of truth until their attention will be attracted so that they will look for the source from which such fragrance comes, and there to their surprise and delight they will see flowers of Pentecost wide open, which, while they gaze, will suddenly fade away and give place to fruitage.

The gifts are for the church and they will make their appearance in their fullness and glory as soon as she is freed from the power and dictations of man, and He to whom she is espoused bears full sway and His laws and orders are fully obeyed in all of her departments.

The teaching must be right, and taught by men who are right; those who measure to the qualifications laid down in the Bible. The lives of the members must be pure and holy. The finances must be gathered and handled properly. The entire Church must be robed in garments of salvation separate from the world and unmixed with selfish motives and ambitions. Behold her as she is drawing nearer. Keep looking until you see her in her original Glory and Power.

> If you'll only look, you'll see
> The Church that gives you liberty;
> Tongues of fire upon you sent,
> And with the glory you'll be content.

> Behold her in her bright array,
> And see her there as plain as day;
> All decked with jewels rich and rare,
> And shining gems so bright and fair.

CHAPTER XV.

THE CHURCH OF GOD, CONTINUED.

When Jesus was preaching to the people He very often used, for illustration, the common things around Him, and taught them largely by comparison.

He would sometimes use the sheep and the shepherd to make His teaching impressive, and would sometimes use the vines and branches. He took the penny at one time to teach the lesson. He used the rulers and laws of the country sometimes. He spake in parables and many ways to impress the truths on the minds of the people.

He would sometimes seem very humble and subdued in spirit, at others He would wax bold and speak as one having authority. He would at one time manifest the lamb like spirit, and at another the lion like spirit would prevail. He was fully able for every occasion, and could fill the requirements under all circumstances. There are still remaining signs and fruits of His life and ministry.

He said to His disciples, "I am the vine and ye are the branches." He also gave the thought that upon them the fruit would appear, because they were the branches.

As we study His teachings and instructions as well as the writings of the Apostles, we infer that He must have said something like this: "I am going away, and upon this rock I'm going to build my Church, which is to take my place when I am gone, and she shall be called my body, but I will still remain the head. She must always be subject to me, and I have left all the laws she needs, and she must not leave off any nor add any more."

We acknowledge that He really did establish His Church, and she showed herself in all her beauty and effulgent glory as she sprang fresh from His hands on the day of Pentecost. He had already said, "Greater works than these shall ye do because I go unto the Father," and sure enough, under the very first sermon after the Church really took His place, three thousand souls were added to the one hundred and twenty. And besides this great ingathering, "The Lord added to the Church daily such as should be saved."

The work spread and grew, and "multitudes both of men and women were added unto the Lord." When the Church (His body) was really manifested and took His place the fruit was seen in abundance. From the church went out the teaching of repentance, as a branch from a tree, and on this branch were people who repented. Another branch was extended from the same body named baptism, another sanctification, another baptism with the Holy Ghost, another feet-washing, etc., etc. From the body (the Church) extended every line of truth and teaching that He had given them. Although His disciples were the branches while He was with them, yet when He went away and the Holy Ghost came upon them they were all baptized into one, and became the body from which all the teachings or commands branched out, and then appeared the fruit. People were converted, sanctified, baptized with the Holy Ghost and healed.

Behold, there stands the full developed tree. First is the trunk, and from the trunk extends the branches, and upon the branches appears the leaves and luscious fruit hanging in great yellow or red clusters. The Church of God is to the gospel or doctrine taught in the Bible as the trunk or body of the tree is to the branches, leaves and fruit.

Where did Martin Luther get the doctrine of justification by faith? From the Church of God as it was given by its members through the Bible. The branch had grown and grown and lengthened out through the "dark ages" until by and by Martin Luther appeared as a cluster of fruit away out on the end of the long branch.

Where did John Wesley get the doctrine of sanctification as a definite and instantaneous experience subsequent to justification? From the Church of God. This branch had also extended away out through the darkness, and finally blossomed with

George Fox, and then fruited heavily in the time of the Wesleys. These two branches have grown and borne much precious fruit ever since.

Where did Dr. Simpson get the doctrine of divine healing? Where did this branch come from? The Church of God. Hundreds, yea thousands have given up physicians, thrown away remedies, wheel chairs and crutches, and have been suspended on this wonderful branch.

Where did Dr. Seamore get the doctrine that he preached in Los Angeles, Cal., a few years ago, that not only stirred that western city and our own beloved America, but also the countries across the deep blue sea, yea, and many parts of the world. Where did he get the doctrine—the baptism with the Holy Ghost and the speaking in other tongues as the Spirit gives utterance as the evidence? From the Church of God. This branch, also, had been reaching out and growing in length until it budded, blossomed, and is to-day filled with delicious fruit. The rich experiences,. the shining faces, the good clean lives, the love for one another and the lost souls of earth, the "Go ye" spirit, tears and sacrifices, all tell the story of this special branch having life and fruitage, although thought to have died long ago and been buried with the Apostles. All these branches have been bearing fruit. Thank God.

But the wonder is that none of these men, who

discovered these wonderful truths, ever crawled back down the branch to discover, if possible, where they started from, and locate the trunk of the tree. But no, they seem to have been so occupied with present surroundings and conditions, and the branches had grown so long, and through the long, long night of the "dark ages," that the darkness was too dense and the task too great. And thus, instead of discovering the trunk of the tree, men went to work and got up articles of faith and creeds, and have tried to make out that these precious truths were doctrines of church so and so. For example: It has been said so often that "Sanctification is a doctrine of the Methodist Church," "Baptism by immersion is a doctrine of the Baptist church," etc., etc. None had been able to see just where the branches sprang from and to what body they were attached.

At last, after centuries of fruitage, the branch of sanctification put forth a little unassuming bud, and other little buds made their appearance about the same time. Finally the fruit appeared, and, as if they wondered and consulted with each other as to where such delicious sap and nourishment could come from, finally this least of all, and the most insignificant and uncouth in appearance, disappeared in the darkness as it went rolling and tumbling and rattling down the bark of the branch, and although

the way was lonely and dark, and the obstructions
thick and hard to penetrate, yet as if determined to
reach the trunk or die, it kept scrambling away until
finally the discovery was made, and sure enough,
not only that special branch was located, but also all
the others, whose tip ends had been bearing fruit,
were located, and found to be fastened to and held
in place by the Church of God.

As the discovery was made a shout pierced
through his soul, and almost before he was aware of
it, he was back again at the end of the branch, shouting at the top of his voice, and leaping and clapping
his hands as he cried, "The Church of God! The
Church of God! From her extends all these precious truths! From her comes all the laws and government we need! Away with your articles of
faith! Away with your creeds! Upon 'this rock'
Jesus built His church, and there it is just like it was,
only it has been hidden from view by the debris of
the 'dark ages,' unbelief, and man made churches
and organizations! Hallelujah! Hallelujah! Glory!
Glory!" And the shouts and cries of joy were taken up by the other fruit, and echoed and re-echoed
until dread consternation seized scores and hundreds
of people who looked on with amazement and wonder.

As we trace every branch of truth it runs us right
back to the Church of God—the body of Christ.

People accept the branch or teaching of repentance, or sanctification, or the baptism with the Holy Ghost evidenced by the speaking with other tongues as the Spirit gives utterance, and divine healing, etc., then why not accept the body upon which each branch rests?   Paul tells us that the Church of God is the pillar and ground of the truth.   Then how can you accept the truth without accepting the Church?   It is like purchasing a house that has no foundation or resting place.   No pillars under it, no ground under it.   These truths that we all-love so well are attached to, and had their origination with Jesus, but when He went away they were all transferred to the Church, and there they remain until this day.

The Church of God that is now making such rapid strides into prominence is not a little new man made affair as men suppose; it is the same original, gigantic Church that blazed out and wrought havoc to Satan's devices and man made Judaism of two thousand years ago.   No wonder people fear her. No wonder people are crying out against her and rising up in opposition to her advance.   She is a monster against which they cannot prevail.   And as she spreads and grows she will tear down men's play houses.   Articles of faith and creeds gotten up by wise? educated men will be shivered to atoms, and like little David took the giant's sword and cut

off the head of him who defied Israel's God, and
held it up bleeding, so that the armies on both sides
could see it, so this little despised church will take
her enemy's sword (the Bible) and sever the heads
(opinions and creeds) of her giant opposers from
their shoulders.

Scriptures are plain, but men's minds are dark-
ened. The honest ones will, however, soon find out
they are fighting against God. They will lay down
their weapons and come unto her. The sons and
daughters of the opposers have already come bend-
ing unto her, which is just what the Scriptures say
they will do. (Isa. 60:14.)

She was opposed, but wonderfully successful
when she appeared "As the morning, fair as the
moon, clear as the sun, and terrible as an army with
banners." (Cant. 6:10.) We expect nothing short
of the original power and glory and success, as she
returns, returns, returns, returns, "As it were the
company of two armies." (Cant. 6:13.) And to
make it more emphatic the margin says, "As it were
the company of Mahanaim," which is, "This is
God's host." (Gen. 32:2.) Who want's to fight
against God's host? Who would rather join our
ranks and have a part in this greatest of all achievements—the proclaiming of the gospel to the ends
of the world and the ushering in of the return of our
Lord, who is the great head of the Church?

The Church is still rising, the light is still shining, and many are seeing the brightness of her rising, and gathering themselves together unto her. People are seeing and flowing together; their hearts are fearing and being enlarged. Prophecy is now being fulfilled, and the glory of God is already resting upon the Church of God in a measure. (Isa. 60:1, 5.)

In conclusion I wish to ask the following questions: If justification, sanctification, the baptism of the Spirit, etc., are really branches or teachings from the original Church, and dependent upon her for a foundation, does it not look like robbery for men to establish or make a church with articles of faith and creeds, and take these branches or teachings from the Church of God and put them in their churches? Does it not look like Nebuchadnezzer taking away the sacred vessels from the house of God at Jerusalem? Does it not look like Belshazzer and a thousand of his lords drinking out of these sacred vessels contrary to the will of God? And is there not already faintly, yea, plainly seen the form of a hand writing on the wall the doom of all those who have taken these sacred commands, branches or teachings that rightfully belong to the Church of God and made them principles or creeds in their own organizations? Is God's wrath going to be held back forever?

Were not those very same vessels carried back from Babylon to Jerusalem and placed in the temple when it was rebuilt? (Ezra 1:7, 11; Ezra 5:15, 16.) Does not this and many other Scriptures teach that these teachings we have mentioned above shall be taken from the common churches of the day, and brought back to the Church of God when she is rebuilt? Allow me to emphatically declare that God has already commenced this work, and will continue to work at it until all will be brought back and placed in their rightful place—the Church of God. And the churches that are so popular now will be void of these graces and teachings, and will resort to man made plans and entertainments to attract their members. Is it not so now in many instances?

CHAPTER XVI.

THE CHURCH OF GOD—CONTINUED.

The Bible Church is still so misunderstood by the majority of the people that we are sure those of our readers who do understand will bear with us if we write yet more extensively about it.

We are very anxious for people to obtain such a clear understanding of it that they will not confuse it with the modern churches. True, the modern churches have some things and some ways and some teachings like that of the Bible Church, but they have added to and taken from until the real Bible plans are not followed. If the Bible plans and teachings were perfectly followed by them, then all would be together instead of being divided into several hundred different organizations.

In the days of the Apostles they were all in fellowship and continued in the Apostles' doctrine, and there was but the one church. We are now advocating a return to the same principles, doctrine, faith, fellowship and oneness that they enjoyed in the beginning of the gospel era. At that time fear came upon every soul, and they had favor with all the people. The gospel spread like "wild-fire," and the messengers were accused of filling Jerusalem with their doctrine and turning the world upside down. It is our purpose to draw the minds of the Christian public back to the original, and this is what we mean by advocating the Church of God.

THE APOSTLES' CREED.

"I believe in God, the Father Almighty, maker of heaven and earth; and in Jesus Christ His only Son our Lord; who was conceived by the Holy Ghost, born of the Virgin Mary, suffered under Pontius Pilate, was crucified, dead, and buried; the third day He rose from the dead; He ascended into Heaven, and sitteth at the right hand of God, the Father Almighty, from whence He shall come to judge the quick and the dead. I believe in the Holy Catholic Church; the communion of saints; the forgiveness of sins; the resurrection of the body; and the life everlasting. Amen."

This is a real imposition on the dear old Apostles who gave their lives and shed their blood for a fact, a truth, rather than for a creed.

It is a fraud, for the Apostles had the message direct from the Lord, therefore it would have been impossible for them to have formed a creed. Peter said they were not following cunningly devised fables. (2 Peter 1:16.) John said their hands had handled Him. (1 John 1:1.) They were with Him and knew Him, so they could not have made a creed.

The first history of the "Apostles' Creed" appears

in the third century in the writings of St. Ambrose, about the time of the beginning of the apostacy. The first creed was taken into the church about that time, and now there are probably a thousand or more. The very moment they formulated a creed and set the church upon it, that very moment it ceased to be the Church of God. In comparison it was like the children of Israel were when Moses was in the mount with God and delayed coming down longer than they anticipated, so in his absence they made an idol (golden calf). When the apostles had all died and the church fell into other hands, those who had not seen the Apostles nor the Christ, they formulated their creed.

Israel said, "Up, make us gods, which shall go before us; for as for this Moses, the man that brought us up out of the land of Egypt, we wot not what has become of him." So, when the Apostles, whose doctrines had been followed so closely, were gone, the people said, "Up, make us creeds, for the Apostles are gone." When Moses came down he destroyed the "calf," and gave them to understand that they should not follow anything but God, and He only must they serve. So we are seeking to destroy creeds and get back on the original solid foundation.

Creeds show that people are a long ways off from God, and only have a mere opinion or hearsay of Him. Israel said they did not know what had become of Moses. To accept a creed, people say they don't know what has become of Christ. The Church of God had no creeds, for they knew that Christ had ascended up where He was before, sitting at the right hand of the Father, waiting till His enemies are made His footstool.

The Church of God to-day knows where Jesus is, or else they show their unbelief in the Bible. Creeds give room for, and express a doubt, but the Bible gives no such room. The Bible is a Book of facts, and if it is accepted as such, there can be no room for creeds. Then we are not trying, "as is supposed," to originate another organization, but we are trying to attract and draw the people away from false systems and creeds back to the original laws and facts that are just as true and positive as when the multitudes had such fellowship and oneness as they continued in the Apostles' doctrine; not the Apostles' creed.

For centuries, men of erudition have been instilling into the minds of the masses these false theories until it is not an easy matter for them to be thrown off, but the Holy Spirit is at the head of this movement, and He will guide into all truth and out of all error.

REFORMATION.

We are truly in a time of reformation. The word "reform" means to return to a former good state. To what good state can we return that would be more satisfactory, and that would bring about better success, than the good state that succeeded in carrying the gospel to every creature under heaven? (Col. 1:23.) It is our purpose to return to the plans and doctrines that God so honored as to confirm it with signs and wonders, and which proved to be so successful.

We are misunderstood, criticised, antagonized and opposed, but what do we care for such opposition, when we have God and His Bible as our comfort and stay. We know this reform is needed just as much as the one started by Martin Luther in the sixteenth century. We are not only seeking or striving to re-establish the doctrine of "Justification by faith," but every part and all of the original doctrine of the Apostles. Who could honestly object to this? Who would want to oppose such a reformation? Surely no lover of Jesus Christ would want to speak or write a word in opposition to this great reform movement. Surely all lovers of Christ and His truth will rush into this last great conflict and battle, and fight for the original creedless Church with all of her original grace, power and glory; for the millions of earth are rapidly dropping into hell because of our inability to reach them, and God will never make us able until we get back to the same truth and doctrine for which all the Apostles gave their lives.

This doctrine is dear to the writer. He knows not what is before him, but his life is to be given for the re-establishment of the Lord's Church, and he expects to use his influence on that line as long as God sees fit to let him remain in this tabernacle. We wish to encourage all who are engaged in this wonderful reformation to be very courageous, and remember as men have hazarded their lives in the past, and many, many lives have been sacrificed for this truth, that we must not be one whit behind them in this greatest of all reformations. Let us be wise as serpents, and bold and zealous. The whole creation is groaning now, and waiting for this very reform to succeed in preparing the way for the return of our Lord.

REVOLUTION.

We acknowledge that the earth in revolving comes back to a certain point about every twenty-four hours, and thus we say the sun rises. The earth is supposed to make a circuit, as it travels in its orbit once every year, thus bringing about the seasons in their order about the same time every year. The entire solar system moves in regular order, and each planet comes to or passes a certain point at a certain period of time. Steamboats, railroad trains and street cars all have a starting place, and all return to the same point again.

When Jesus and His Apostles began publishing the gospel, it was accompanied with signs and wonders, as they taught the full gospel, which embraced divine healing for the body and the baptism with the Holy Ghost with the speaking in other tongues as the evidence, as well as the other teachings that are more common. For nearly twenty centuries the great wheel of time has been slowly revolving, until the cycle is almost complete. If this argument is true, and we have many good reasons to believe it is, then when the cycle is really complete we may expect the same results when the enormous cylinder was put in motion.

The time for the restitution of all things is at hand. Jesus said He was the beginning and the ending, so as He was in the beginning, and His was the only Church recognized and known and in existence, and His the only doctrine taught, so the same is now returning. That we are now on the very verge of a complete revolution and change in religious affairs is evident. Things cannot go on long as they are. Everything is in a strain. The tensions are tightened to their utmost capacity. Churches and mission boards and church benevolent institutions have gone almost to the extreme limit. Many of their members are refusing to pay their dues because they feel they are receiving no spiritual food. Ministers are giving up their circuits and parishes because of a shortness of funds.

Not a few houses, whose walls used to echo the shouts of happy, well fed souls, are left for the owls and bats. Lodges and shows, base-ball games and theaters, society and dress parades are attracting the once happy church going people and commanding their money. The most spiritual among the churches are wandering about for soul food, and of course they naturally fall into the Pentecostal meetings, and the result of such rambles is that soon they receive the baptism with the Holy Ghost and begin to talk in tongues, and then they are ruined for their church and their church for them, so they look around for a church home; and as soon as the Bible Church is presented to them they see it, and in they go. A revolution? Yes, we are more into it than many are able to comprehend, but it is getting more and more comprehensive as time flies by.

The minds of the members of the popular churches are changing so rapidly now that the pastors are unable to keep up with them, and all their efforts to hold them are futile. The revolution is upon us, and we had just as well acknowledge it. There will soon be but two forces: one for Christ and His Church, the other for the antichrist. Which side will you take? Then move quickly, for the last great conflict is on, and you will soon be compelled, by a force of circumstances which will be irresistible, to take one side or the other.

When Israel had wandered away from the commandments of God and had gone to worshiping idols, Joshua called them together and said, "Now therefore fear the Lord, and serve him in sincerity and in truth: and put away the gods which your fathers served, * * * * and serve ye the Lord. And if it seem evil unto you to serve the Lord, choose you this day whom you will serve; * * * * but as for me and my house, we will serve the Lord." (Josh. 24:14, 15.) Before this last great conflict is ended every one will be compelled to choose which they will serve, Christ or antichrist. Choose Christ to-day, before you unconsciously receive the mark of the beast in your right hand or in your forehead.

CHAPTER XVII.

PREVAILING PRAYER.

As it is our desire and purpose for this book to stimulate and inspire its readers to redouble their energy and efforts to forward the gospel and win the victory in this last great conflict, we feel it would hardly be complete without a chapter on prayer.

Prevailing prayer implies and embodies all works, as the seed embodies the trunk, root, branches, flowers and fruitage of the tree.

The history of piety is the history of prayer. All piety and successful Christian work begins, continues and ends with prayer. From the offering of Abel's acceptable sacrifice down to the present moment, all blessings of grace have been bestowed in answer to the triple intercessions of the Son of God, the Holy Spirit and believing souls.

The angel said to Jacob (Gen. 32:28), "As a prince hast thou power with God and with men and hast prevailed." If, by the effort of prayer, we may prevail, both with God and with men, is there anything else we can do in life which, in importance and power, is equal to prayer? On the day of Pentecost the preacher and the whole church being full of faith, the Holy Ghost, and power, in answer to the prayer of faith, one sermon resulted in the conversion of three thousand souls. To-day three thousand sermons without this power in answer to prayer, would not save one sinner. The more of churches and sermons we have without prayer that brings an enduement of power, the worse are we off. They are a savor of death unto death, and as some one has said: "If there was a religion to-day that had the doctrine and all the ordinances of the New Testament, and yet, without the baptism of the Holy Ghost, it would not be Christianity."

Because of the interests pending, and the power God has placed at the disposal of him who prays, the most interesting sight in this world is a man in the act of prayer. The angels of God look with wonder, and the Lord of angels bends from His lofty throne and exclaims, "Behold, he prayeth!"

God has revealed the necessity of prayer and its almost unlimited power. "Ask and it shall be given you." "If ye shall ask anything in my name, I will do it." Prayer is intimately associated with man's salvation, and without it we cannot be saved.

How much in Christian experience and Christian labor, depends on prayer! Without prayer for the power of the Holy Ghost to attend the truth preached, the Word will be a dead letter. "The letter killeth but the Spirit giveth life." No wonder there are so many dead formal churches. It is the unction that makes the preacher.

How did Fletcher and Finney get this unction? By praying without ceasing, by pleading, wrestling, and prevailing at a throne of grace. All great soul winners have conquered on their knees. Without prevailing prayer the meetings become as cold as death, and the churches will dwindle and become extinct. What is wanting in so many instances, is the power of the Holy Ghost to move and act in answer to the effectual, fervent prayer of the saints of God.

The Spirit of God is the great agent, who is the source of all vitality and power in every service. His life and power are given in answer to the prayer of faith, and never otherwise. How did the early church get such great power? What could they have done without it? What did they do with it? What can we do without it? A writer says of the sainted Bramwell: "I attribute the greater portion of his success in the ministry to his diligence and prayer."

As we advance we see in prayer the great means for obtaining strength and wisdom for our work in the Lord's service. As we understand this subject, we will see more and more that intercessory prayer is the most important and the most real work the

Christian has to do. "And I sought for a man among them, that should make up the hedge, and stand in the gap before me for the land that I should not destroy it, but I found none. Therefore I poured out mine indignation upon them; I have consumed them with the fire of my wrath; their own way have I recompensed upon their heads, saith the Lord God." (Ezek. 22:30, 31.) What a responsible position we occupy! To stand in the gap in intercessory prayer for the salvation of souls, to keep off the wrath of God is the need of the hour.

Prevailing prayer leads us into a holy and intimate nearness to God. It is the only way to God, the only medium of communion with Him. Prevailing with God is the secret of prevailing with men, and must precede it. On what we transact with God at a throne of grace depends what we may accomplish with men. We may pray, sing and preach until we drop into our graves, but until we prevail all will go for nothing. It is one thing to pray, and another thing to prevail in prayer.

Esau was conquered while Jacob wrestled until the break of day. The lions' mouths were closed while Daniel was on his knees. Elijah prayed, "And it rained not for the space of three years and six months." He prayed again, "and it came to pass, in the meanwhile, that the heavens were black

with clouds, and wind, and there was a great rain."
When the Israelites had made them a golden calf
and worshipped it, God determined to destroy them,
and said to Moses: "I have seen this people, and,
behold, it is a stiff-necked people: Now, therefore,
let me alone, that my wrath may wax hot against
them, and that I may consume them: and I will
make of thee a great nation. And Moses besought
the Lord, his God, and said, Lord, why doth thy
wrath wax hot against thy people?   *   *   *   *
Turn from thy fierce wrath, and repent of this evil
against thy people.   *   *   *   *   And the Lord repented of the evil which he thought to do unto his
people." But for the prayer of Moses, God would
have annihilated the whole nation instead of cutting
off but a few thousand of the idolaters. Strange as
it may seem, yet the life of a nation depended on
the prayer of faith offered by Moses.

> "Oh, wonderful power of faithful prayer!
> What tongue can tell the almighty grace?
> God's hands are bound or open are,
> As Moses or Elijah prays!
> Let Moses in the Spirit groan;
> And God cries out, 'Let me alone.' "

When Haman sought revenge on all the Jews in
all the realms of Ahasuerus, because of the insult
tendered him by Mordecai the Jew, and when it

was decreed by the king that all the Jews should be put to death, Mordecai informed queen Esther of the bloody plot; and the queen bade Mordecai: "Go, gather together all the Jews that are present in Shushan, and fast ye for me; and neither eat nor drink three days, night or day: I also and my maidens will fast likewise, and so will I go in unto the king, which is not according to the law: and if I perish, I perish."

When the Jews had thus, for three days and nights, fasted and prayed, God answered and delivered them, and destroyed their enemy. He who prays in faith enlists almighty God, all the armies of heaven and every law of the universe, in the interest of his cause.

Strange as it may seem, nevertheless, the eternal salvation of the lost depends on God's people at a throne of grace. It is in answer to prevailing prayer that power is given to move the lost to accept Christ. Peter was released from prison while the church at Jerusalem were on their knees. It was the power of the Holy Ghost, given in answer to the prayer of faith, that made the truth in Peter's sermon, on the day of Pentecost, effectual in the conviction and conversion of three thousand souls. Without this power in answer to prayer, the multitude would have remained unmoved, except that probably they

would have become so enraged that Peter would
have lost his life.   The prayer of faith brought a
power that enchained the rabble and subdued the
otherwise invincible.

It was the power of God that came while Paul
and Silas prayed and sang praises to God, that made
the earth quake and sinners tremble, and that opened
the prison door and wicked hearts as well.   The
power that did these things centuries ago, can do the
same to-day.   This power is given to us in answer
to the prayer of faith.

The Syro-Phoenician woman, whose daughter
was a demoniac, cried out of her maternal heart:
"Have mercy on me, O Lord, thou Son of David,
*   *   *   * Lord help me!"   To which Christ
responded, "O woman, great is thy faith: be it unto
thee even as thou wilt."   And her daughter was
made whole from that very hour.   The all important thing for that mother to do was to believe—prevail.

The all important thing for us to do in these days,
is to believe—to have great faith in God, and this
comes of great praying.

The death warrant of "Bloody Mary" was signed
in heaven, while John Knox was on his knees, saying: "Give me Scotland or I die."   When that
wicked ruler said: "I fear the prayers of John Knox

more than I fear all the armies of Europe," she paid the finest tribute to the power of prayer to be found on the pages of history.   The Emperor of Germany resolved to proclaim religious toleration throughout his realm, while Martin Luther and some of his helpers were on their knees: when Luther exclaimed: "Deliverance has come!   Deliverance has come!"

Without the quickening and convicting operations of the Holy Ghost, the sinner will not, cannot come to God.   These operations of the Holy Ghost are conditioned on the faith of the children of God.   As the saints prevail with God for the convicting power of the Holy Ghost upon sinners, the responsibility for the salvation of sinners is transferred from the Christians to sinners themselves.   Only where Christians have done their utmost, is the responsibility entirely transferred to sinners.   Then how great, how charming the responsibility of Christians! Then how important this subject of prayer in this time of the last great conflict!

As priests, we must go into the holy of holies of God's presence by the way of prayer, and receive "all the fullness of God" ourselves, and answer for the salvation of others, and then return to the people with a blessing for them.   Christ spent a whole night on the mountain in prayer, that the next day He might return "in the power of the Spirit," with great blessings for the people.

How marvelous the power the church may wield at the throne of grace to move the "Lord of the harvest to send forth more laborers into His vineyard," to carry "this gospel of the kingdom in all the world for a witness" in this generation! The gathering of the harvest depends on prayer. How solemn the thought! How almost overwhelming the sense of responsibility that thrills the soul of him who understands the power of prayer, and is in sympathy with a lost race in its paramount peril, and with Him who "gave His life a ransom for all," as he lifts his eyes and sees "the fields already white unto the harvest!"

No subject equals in importance this subject. By prayer we receive of God's life and take on His character. We become like those with whom we have continuous and loving fellowship.

"We shall be like Him, for we shall see Him as He is." We now behold Him in the gospel glass face to face, and are "changed into the same image, from glory to glory, even as by the Spirit of the Lord." "As He (Jesus) prayed, the fashion of His countenance was altered, and His raiment was white and glistering." And the fashion of our countenances will be changed as we draw near to God in prayer.

Then pray for Jesus' sake!   Pray for the salvation of the lost!   Pray for your own present good and eternal glory!   Pray now, while we are in this last great conflict, for by prayer only will the victory be won and the conflict ended, and Jesus reign supreme. Pray!   Pray!!   Pray!!!

banks and nations have plans for business intercourse, making their exchanges with system and order.

Jesus said, "The children of this world are in
their generation wiser than the children of light,"
but He did not say it should be so. God, through
the mouth of the prophet Hosea, said, "My people
are destroyed for lack of knowledge," but He did
not say it should be so, neither did He say we
should not search for, and obtain, the necessary
knowledge that would preserve us. God, through
the prophet Isaiah said, "For as the heavens are
higher than the earth, so are my ways higher than your
ways," but He did not say we should not learn His
ways. Paul said, "Eye hath not seen, nor ear heard,
neither have entered into the heart of man, the things
which God hath prepared for them that love him.
But God hath revealed them unto us by His Spirit:
for the Spirit searcheth all things, yea, the deep things
of God." So it is evidently God's will for these
hidden treasures and gems of truth to be unearthed
and utilized for our good and His glory.

Hundreds of thousands of honest souls are searching for the truths hidden away in the Bible, and realizing great spiritual gain by the required sacrifice
and toil. Not a few have accepted the tithing
system, and some are advocating the practice of
selling their possessions and laying the proceeds at

the Apostles' feet, as was done by the early Church in Judea, while still others claim we should not have any special system, but every one should give as he purposes in his own heart, much or little, and anywhere he wishes.

In the glaring light that beams upon the Bible when the Holy Ghost illuminates its pages, our ways have many times appeared very crude and immature. No doubt the time will come when we will see our imperfections in handling the Lord's money. The Bible teaches order and system about other things; why not about money matters? We have learned many things by types and shadows; it is surely not improbable that we can learn something about the money system in the same way. The Holy Scriptures surely teach a money system, so we would do well to search for it. True, it is not always called money, but generally its equivalent is the term used in its types and shadows.

The tithe is first mentioned in the Bible at Gen. 14:20, where the account is given of Abram returning from the slaughter of the kings and met Melchisedek, "the priest of the most high God," and Abram "gave him tithes of all" the spoil he had taken in battle, and Melchisedek blessed him. At Gen. 28:22 is the closing of the narrative of Jacob's vow to God about 153 years later, where he said, "If God will be with me, and will keep me in this way that I go, and will give me bread to eat, and raiment to put on, so that I come again to my father's house in peace; then shall the Lord be my God: And this stone, which I have set for a pillar, shall be God's house: And of all that thou shalt give me I will surely give the tenth unto thee."

We do not read of God ever giving Abram and Jacob any command to pay tithes, but it seemed to be voluntary on their part, but in each case the giver received a blessing. While there is no history showing that God had commanded these, his servants, to pay tithes, yet 269 years after, when the law was given, the tithing system was instituted and placed in the law, as if it was something of importance. In the law is given the tithing system, and from that time tithing was practiced and mentioned by the prophets, and that subject is taken up in the New Testament and emphasized.

While the law was a schoolmaster to bring Israel to Christ (Gal. 3:24), and that law was until John (Luke 16:16), and Christ is the end of the Law for righteousness (Rom. 10:4) yet it is spoken of as "having a shadow of good things to come" (Heb. 10:1), and is acknowledged to typify the gospel or grace dispensation. There can be no shadow without a real body, and a light on the other side opposite the shadow. Enter the shadow of a tree at the extreme point farthest from it and move toward the light, and yet keep the tree between you and the light, and you will remain in the shadow until you reach the tree itself. Mark out the shadow and raise it up perpendicular, and you have the shape of the tree looking from one side. Now we are to learn something about the body by the shadow—we are to learn something about the antitype by the type: We want to make out the shape of the shadow, raise it up perpendicular, and look at it so closely that we will be able to see God's great money sys-tem intended for the last days, and put it into prac-tice, along with the other hidden treasures that are being brought to light and experienced.

The Levites were to have no inheritance among the other tribes of Israel, but were to have charge of the tabernacle service and worship. (Num. 18:23.) "The tithes of the children of Israel, which they offer as an offering unto the Lord," were given to the Levites. (Num. 18:24.) Then when they received the tithes of Israel they were to tithe the tithes as an offering to the Lord. And the Lord's heave offering was given to Aaron the priest. (Num. 18:26, 28.)

The writer of Hebrews, who was no doubt per-fectly informed about the law, and God's financial plan, throws some light on the subject. First, he mentions "Melchisedec, * * * * priest of the most high God, who met Abraham returning from the slaughter of the kings and blessed him; to whom also Abraham gave a tenth part of all." (Heb. 7:1, 2.) Then as if to emphasize the importance of paying tithes he still holds us back before the time the law was given, and insists on a consideration of this subject, and says: "Now consider how great this man was, unto whom even the patriarch Abraham gave a tenth of the spoils." (Heb. 7:4.) This is as much as to say that if there was nothing in the paying of tithes this great man, Melchisedec, would not have received them, neither would Abraham, the friend of God, have given them.

Now let us notice his argument a little further: "And verily they that are of the sons of Levi, who received the office of the priesthood, have a commandment to take tithes of the people according to the law, that is, of their brethren, though they came out of the loins of Abraham: But he whose descent is not counted from them received tithes of Abraham, and blessed him that had the promises. And without all contradiction the less is blessed of the better." (Heb. 7:5-7.) The argument here is conclusive. The tithing system was inaugurated before the law came, and was conducted properly. Here then is where it originated. The tithes were paid to him "of whom it is witnessed that he liveth." (Heb. 7:8.) The law was only the type, and "Was added because of transgressions, till the seed should come to whom the promise was made." (Gal. 3:19.) Then when the seed came, the plan was to continue after the original order. Christ, our high priest, was "made an high priest forever after the order of Melchisedec," (Heb 6:20), "and not * * called after the order of Aaron." Then the tithing system is not to be adopted because of the commands of the law, but as we have now come to the time for perfect order, it is to be practiced because of a connection, through Christ, with the perfect order. The law was a link thrown in to occupy the time until the seed came, and all the time of the law, even that was given as a type to teach that there was something better ahead. A counterfeit coin could not be a counterfeit except there was a genuine coin. There could be no type if there was nothing for it to represent.

During the age of the types they were commanded to pay tithes, but in the beginning of tithe paying, history shows it was only voluntary, but recived the approval of him "of whom it is witnessed that he liveth." "We are not under law, but under grace" (Rom. 6:14), but are we to transgress "because we are not under the law, but under grace? God forbid." (Rom. 6:15.) The law says, "Thou shalt not

kill," but under grace we will not kill. Under the
law they were commanded to pay tithes, but under
grace we will pay tithes. "The law made nothing
perfect" (Heb. 7:19); of course not, for perfection is
only brought about by glad, free, voluntary service
as soon as the requirements are known. Nothing
said about Abraham being compelled to pay tithes,
but he did it and received the blessing. Nothing
said about Abraham being compelled to offer his
son Isaac as a sacrifiice, but early the next morning
he started out to do it. No murmur, no complaint,
no objection raised. God said it, and that was
enough.

We have already shown that those who received
tithes were to also pay tithes. Thus the children of
Israel were to pay tithes to the Levites, and they
were to tithe the tithes and pay their tithes to Aaron
the priest. Thus showing a system similar to our
tax system in the United States of America. The
people pay their taxes to the county, and a certain
per cent goes to the State, and the balance is used
in the county. Then a certain per cent goes to the
national government, and the balance remains to be
used for State expenses. This gives an example of
a systematic arrangement.

Under the great reformation conducted by Ezra
and Nehemiah, which is a type of the reformation
now upon us, they did not neglect the money mat-

ters, for they appointed treasurers over the treasuries, and all Judah brought their tithes (not money, but products of the land) into the treasuries (Neh. 13:10-13), then distribution was made in systematic order.

When God was calling for a return of His people unto Himself through the mouth of His prophet Malachi, He said: "Will a man rob God? Yet ye have robbed me. But ye say, wherein have we robbed thee? In tithes and offerings. * * * * Bring ye all the tithes into the storehouse, that there may be meat in mine house, and prove me now herewith, saith the Lord of hosts, if I will not open you the windows of heaven, and pour you out a blessing, that there shall not be room enough to receive it." (Mal. 3;8, 10.)

CHAPTER XIX.

In the preceding chapter we have considered the system with but little reference to the New Testament. We now take up the subject to continue it by weaving more New Testament Scriptures into the discussion.

The last Scriptures used in the former chapter emphasized the importance of having money in the treasury. This same teaching is confirmed by the actions or practice of the early church. "Neither was there any among them that lacked: for as many as were possessors of lands or houses sold them, and brought the prices of the things that were sold, and laid them down at the apostles' feet; and distribution was made unto every man according as he had need. And Joses * * * * having land, sold it, and brought the money, and laid it at the apostles' feet." (Acts 4:34-37.)

Paul at 1 Cor. 16:1, 2, gives us a hint of about the same thing, but it makes each individual his own treasurer, but orders that the money be placed in a position that it will be ready for use without having to gather it when it is to be used. "Now concerning the collection for the saints, as I have given orders to the churches of Galatia, even so do ye.

Upon the first day of the week let every one of you lay by him in store, as God has prospered him, that there be no gatherings when I come." It is evident that there was to be a collection, and yet no gatherings when Paul came. Then if there was to be no gatherings when he came, it surely would not be out of order to suppose that they were expected to put it all together in a treasury so it would be ready when Paul came for it.

Now to drop back to our pattern, Jesus, it is easy to see He endorsed having a treasury. He only had twelve men with Him as close followers, and yet they had a treasury, for it is written, "Judas had the bag."

"And Jesus sat over against the treasury, and beheld how the people cast money into the treasury: and many who were rich cast in much. * * * * This poor widow hath cast more in, than all they which have cast into the treasury." (Mark 14:41-44.) In these and other Scriptures where Jesus had to do with the treasury, there is no record given that He condemned it, therefore we can conclude that He endorsed the plan.

When Jesus was preaching to the people He spoke out directly to the Pharisees and said: "For ye tithe mint and rue and all manner of herbs, and pass over judgment and the love of God: these ought ye to have done, and not to leave the other undone."

(Luke 11:42.) In this can be seen that He was endorsing both tithing and the treasury, for to pay tithes at that time meant having a treasury.

Referring again to the early church, it is fully demonstrated in the sixth chapter of Acts that they had a treasury, and seven men were appointed and ordained to have charge of the public funds. This common fund was not only to be used for expenses and evangelism, but to supply the temporal needs of every one under the care of the church. In fact there is nothing given that shows any of this was used for evangelistic purposes except that every man's need was supplied, and there was no lack. The inference is that it was used for whatever demands were to be met.

There is nothing written in the book of Acts about paying tithes, but there is written therein about many selling their possessions and putting the receipts into a common treasury, over which the seven deacons were placed. It is not written that they were required by the church to do this, but it was voluntary on their part.

At 2 Cor. 9:7, Paul writes about the same subject of voluntary giving. It might be all of one's possessions or only a part, but every one must give, and the preceding verse advises giving bountifully.

There is the subject of tithing and also that of giving. In the law, which is the type, there were the tithes and the voluntary offerings besides. They were required to pay the tithes: this must be done, and of the first fruits, too. Then the voluntary offerings followed in proportion to their desires and abilities.

With Abraham commenced the tithing, and he gave his tithes to Melchisedec, priest of the most high God. Jesus became the high priest after the order of Melchisedec the same as if the law had never existed. The law was added because of transgressions (Gal. 3:19), and was a schoolmaster to bring us to Christ (Gal. 3:24), that we might get back to the original line of priesthood, "Not after the law of a carnal commandment, but after the power of an endless life."

Having been in the shadow so long, and having been groping along in the dark up till the body that made the shadow was past, is it any wonder that the early church broke out in the brilliancy and flood of light, and did not stop with tithes and offerings, but gave all their possessions? Abraham volunteered the giving of the tithes to Melchisedec, so the members of the early church, after bursting out from the shadow, voluntarily gave all their possessions.

To whom did the members of the early church give their possessions? Was it to the poor, or to the missionaries, or evangelists, or orphanages, or charity homes? No, to none of these. If not to the poor, nor to missions, nor evangelists, nor homes for the widows and orphans, then to whom did they give their possessions?

Abraham gave to Melchisedec in person. In the time of the early church Jesus was high priest after the order of Melchisedec. Jesus Himself, the head of the church, had ascended to the Father, but the church, which is His body, was on earth, and the apostles were the officers of the church, then it is easily seen that all the offerings were laid at the apostles' feet, as that was the only way to give literally to the High Priest. The offerings must be made to the High Priest who was after the order of Melchisedec. The church, then, was His body. (Eph. 1:22, 23, and Col. 1:18.) All literal offerings were made to His body, the church, of which the apostles were chief. This was following the order in which Abraham gave a tenth of the spoils to Melchisedec. This was as though the law had never been. They were not under the law, but under grace. (Rom. 6:14). Abraham was not under the law, for he was before the law, but he gave the tenth of all before the law came.

If Abraham gave a tenth of his spoils before the law came, would it be reason to expect people to give any less after the law was ended? Remember the law was a schoolmaster, teaching in types and shadows, and Abraham had no such training.

The early Christians proved that no less than a tenth should be given, and also proved their willingness to give more than the tithe, and they gave directly to the church instead of scattering it around promiscuously, as is the case with people who give in these days.

The law, our schoolmaster, has taught us, then, that tithes and offerings should be made to our High Priest—Jesus, for whom His body, the church, stands in His place. The priests and Levites received the tithes and offerings from all Israel in the tabernacle service, and they were called "the church in the wilderness." The members of the early church made their offerings to the church in direct harmony with the type. After these offerings were placed in the treasury, then distribution was made proportionately as every one had need.

By this time surely every one who has followed us closely can see the mistakes of recent years by those who have been paying tithes and offerings. They have been throwing them out here and there as they felt led to do, and probably under the existing circumstances it has been the best that could have been done, but it is now evident that God has a wiser plan, a better way, a perfect money system to be put into practice for these last days. It is certainly plain that tithes and offerings should be placed or paid into the Church, His body, and distribution

made to supply the demands in all places and for
all purposes.

We are indeed in the last great conflict, and the
money system is no little factor in it. It is on conditions that all tithes be brought into the storehouse
until there is a surplus on hands that the windows
of heaven are to be opened and blessings poured
out to such an extent that there will not be room
enough to receive them.   The members of the early
church made all their offerings to the church, His
body, and what happened then?   Read the first
chapters of Acts, and you can see that the windows
of heaven were wide open and multitudes were
added to the Lord.

Christ's body, His church, has been ignored, and
God is not well pleased with it, and thus leanness of
soul and poverty among the members is the result.   "Bring ye all the tithes into the storehouse,
that there may be meat in mine house, and prove
me now herewith, saith the Lord of hosts, if I will
not open the windows of heaven, and pour you out
a blessing, that there shall not be room enough to
receive it."   (Mal. 3:10.)   Where are the tithes to
be placed?   "Oh, just anywhere," is the answer
given by hundreds according to their weekly practice.   "Just so I pay the tithes, it don't make any
difference where or to whom I give them.   I want
some to go to foreign missions, and some to home

missions, and some to the poor." Yes, and as you
have been doing this hasn't your souls become
leaner and leaner, and are you not wondering what
is the matter with you? The fact of the matter is
that by throwing your tithes out hither and thither
out of God's plan closes the windows tighter and
tighter, until you can scarcely breathe any spiritual
atmosphere. "Where then should my tithes and offerings go?" I answer, by the authority of God's
Word both in types and shadows and apostolic practices, they should be given into the church. "That
there may be meat in mine house." Must have a
surplus in the treasury to prove the Lord and see if
He will open the windows of heaven and pour out
the abundant blessings. Where is a church that has
a surplus in the treasury? But I'll show you one
that had and the blessings fell. Study the early
church. See how she grew and spread.

Listen at Paul as he gave instructions to the Co-
rinthians. "Now therefore perform the doing of it;
that as there was a readiness to will, so there may
be a performance also out of that which ye have.
For if there be first a willing mind, it is accepted
according to that a man hath, and not according to
that he hath not. For I mean not that other men
be eased, and ye burdened: But by an equality,
that now at this time your abundance may be a supply for their want, that their abundance also may be

a supply for your want: that there may be equality: as it is written, He that had gathered much had nothing over; and he that had gathered little had no lack." (2 Cor. 8:11-15.)

"Now of the things we have written this is the sum: We have an high priest, who is set on the right hand of the throne of the Majesty in the heavens; A minister of the sanctuary, and of the true tabernacle, which the Lord pitched, and not man," who is the head of the church, and His church is His body, to whom we should bring our tithes and offerings.

To make it plain I give a practical plan or system, as I gather it from the teachings of Scripture. The Scriptures have been carefully searched and studied on this particular subject, and the plan has gradually developed in my mind for more than three years, but this is the first time I have ventured to place it before the public in its fullness. It is not meant to strictly follow the system according to the territory shown, but for our own country it would probably not be far wrong.

THE SYSTEM OUTLINED.

Every member of every local church should pay tithes of all his earnings and offerings as he purposes in his own heart; and every church should have a treasury (deacons) to receive all the tithes and offerings, and the treasurer should keep a strict account of every cent received and every cent paid out, and for what purpose. One-tenth of all receipts should be advanced to the State treasury, who in turn should advance a tenth of all he receives to the general treasury. Every treasury should have an advisory council or cabinet, composed of not less than three for the local church, five for the State treasury and seven for the general treasury.

These treasurers and counselmen should measure to the requirements, given by the Bible, for deacons. They should perform their duties in the fear of God, with love, wisdom and discretion.

The funds kept in the local treasury should be used for local expenses first. The pastor should receive his share; then the incidental expenses of the church, extra evangelists, the poor, the sick, and in case of the death of a member whose relatives are not able, to give such a decent burial. All these should have attention and their needs supplied. If the church prospers and there is but little local expenses to be met, and there is a surplus of funds, some could be offered to the State or general treasuries, or used to send their own members who might be called as evangelists or missionaries and support them. There should always be kept a little surplus in the treasury, "that there may be meat in mine house." (Mal. 3:10.)

The funds in the State treasury should be used to

extend the church and evangelism in the State, and assist local churches that are not able to meet their expenses because of misfortunes, such as sickness, deaths, loss by fire, etc. It would not be out of order to establish State institutions, such as schools and orphanages, when the supply of means is sufficient and the demand great enough.

The funds in the general or supreme treasury should be used to extend the gospel and church into new fields, and appropriations could be made to particular localities, where they are in special straits on account of poverty caused by sickness, death, persecutions or famine.

A surplus of funds should always be kept in all the treasuries, so there could be ready money to meet special unexpected demands, without having to go to collecting, as is the case usually. Poor members of the church should always be provided for out of the local funds first, in case of accident, sickness or death in the family, and in case the local treasury is not sufficient, application should be made to the higher treasuries.

When this system is in full working order with every member in every church lovingly and gladly, freely and bountifully giving of their tithes and offerings into the church, the body of Christ, then we may expect God to do great things, and "The people that do know their God shall be strong, and do exploits," and this world will soon be evangelized, the last battle fought, the victory won and the last great conflict ended.

CHAPTER XX.

About the year 1884, a spirit of dissatisfaction and unrest began to work in the mind of a licensed minister of the Missionary Baptist Church by the name of Richard G. Spurling, then living in Monroe county, Tenn. The dissatisfaction arose because of certain traditions and creeds which were burdensome and exceedingly binding on the members.

This humble and sincere servant of God, who was also a faithful servant of the church of which he was a member and licensed minister, began a more careful study of the Bible, and for two years or more spent much time in searching the Scriptures and church history, with a view to a reformation.

After two years or more of careful searching, praying and weeping, and pleading with his church for reform to no avail, he, with others, began to arrange for an independent meeting for a conference and a more careful consideration of religious matters.

The result of the prayers and research on the part of Mr. Spurling and his companions proved three things to their entire satisfaction.

In the sixteenth and seventeenth centuries, when the noble and illustrious reformers were throwing off and breaking out from under the galling yoke of Romanism, and launched and inaugurated what is commonly known as Protestantism, they failed to reform from creeds; they adopted the law of faith when they should have adopted the law of love; and third, they failed to reserve a right of way for the leadership of the Holy Ghost and conscience.

Besides the aforesaid points, they were awakened to the fact that God's church only existed where His law and government was observed by His children.

After having taken plenty of time for consideration, the time and place for the meeting was arranged and announced. That day is worthy of remembrance. Thursday, August 19, 1886.

The small company of humble, faithful, conscientious pilgrims met at Barney Creek meeting house, Monroe county, Tennessee. After prayer, a strong discourse was delivered by Richard G. Spurling, emphasizing the need of a reformation. The arguments were full of force and proved effective, and were endorsed by the hearers, so that when the time came for action there was free and earnest response.

The proposition and obligation was simple. We give it below: "As many Christians as are here present that are desirous to be free from all men made creeds and traditions, and are willing to take the New Testament, or law of Christ, for your only rule of faith and practice; giving each other equal rights and privilege to read and interpret for yourselves as your conscience may dictate, and are willing to set together as the Church of God to transact business at the same, come forward."

In response to this proposition eight persons, whose names are given below, presented themselves and gave to each other the right hands of fellowship: Richard Spurling, John Plemons, Sr., Polly Plemons, Barbara Spurling, Margaret Lauftus, Melinda Plemons, John Plemons, Jr., Adeline Lauftus.

After having joined themselves together under the above obligation they decided to name the baby organization "Christian Union." They then decided to receive persons into membership who were possessed with a good Christian character, and that ordained and licensed ministers from other churches could retain their same position or office without being reordained.

By virtue of the office he had held as a faithful ordained minister in the Missionary Baptist Church for a number of years, Elder Richard Spurling was duly acknowledged and recognized as their minister, to do all the business devolved on him as such in the new order. He then having been placed in authority by the body, took his seat as moderator, and by prayer dedicated the infant church to God, imploring His guidance and blessings for it, and that it might grow and prosper, and accomplish great good.

An invitation was then given for the reception of members, and they received Richard G. Spurling, who was then a licensed minister. The church chose him as their pastor, and had him ordained the next month, September 26, 1886.

Soon after this, Elder Richard Spurling died, at the advanced age of about seventy-four years. Although he was honored with being the first ordained minister, yet he did not live to see the results of his prayers, tears and labors of love in assisting to launch this last great reformation, that is now assuming such vast proportions as it is spreading over the world.

To the sleepless nights of prayer and labors of love by this remarkable old saint and his son, Richard G. Spurling, who is still living, we attribute much of the success and advancement of later years. No doubt they only saw the light as through a glass darkly, but the rays of the early dawn pierced through the darkness until they were made able to at least declare independence and freedom from creeds and sing "Hosannah to the Son of David" for liberty. Great praises be to our God.

The little church grew very slow. But few cared anything about the infant organization. The pastor, R. G. Spurling, continued his preaching, not only at the church, but wherever he was granted the liberty.

In this way the minds of the people were continually agitated, and gradually prepared for the work of the Spirit that was to follow. For ten years this servant of God prayed, wept and continued his ministry against much opposition and under peculiar difficulties, before seeing much fruits of his labor.

In the year 1896 three men, who lived in the same county and locality, became much enthused religiously, and were powerfully wrought on by the Spirit of God. These men, whose names were William Martin, Joe M. Tipton and Milton McNabb, went over into Cherokee county, North Carolina, and commenced a meeting at the Schearer school house. They preached a clean gospel, and urged the people to seek and obtain sanctification subsequent to justification. They prayed, fasted and wept before the Lord until a great revival was the result. People became interested, and were stirred for miles around. Quite a large number professed salvation and sanctification through the blood of Christ. The Baptist and Methodist churches became antagonistic to the wonderful revival that was spreading, and about thirty were excluded from the Baptist church at one time because they professed to live a holy life, which the church denounced as heresy.

After the close of the series of meetings, and the three evangelists were gone, the people commenced a Sunday School, and regular prayer meetings were conducted, usually by William F. Bryant, a leading man of the community. The people earnestly sought God, and the interest increased until unexpectedly, like a cloud from a clear sky, the Holy Ghost began to fall on the honest, humble, sincere seekers after God. While the meetings were in progress one after another fell under the power of God, and soon quite a number were speaking in other tongues as the Spirit gave them utterance. The influence and excitement then spread like wildfire, and people came for many miles to investigate, hear and see the manifestations of the presence of God.

Men, women and children received the Holy Ghost and spoke in other tongues under the power of the mighty Spirit of God.

The power of healing was soon realized, and a number of miraculous cases of healings were wrought by the power of God. The people knew but little about the Bible, but they prayed, and shouted and exhorted until hundreds of hard sinners were converted. The influence grew and spread until it extended into three or four adjoining counties. Persecutions arose, and four or five houses were burned where these earnest, humble people met for worship.

At one time the storm of persecution broke in with such fury that one hundred and six men, composed of Methodist and Baptist ministers, stewards and deacons, one justice of the peace and one sheriff, banded themselves together to put down the revival, even by violence, if that was the only way it could be accomplished. They deliberately tore down and burned the house, where sinners were getting saved in nearly every service, in open daylight. But the greater the persecution the more the revival spread.

The meetings were moved to the home of W. F. Bryant, and the power and glory increased. It was while they were in progress there that seven men banded themselves together to stop the work, and one day rode to the home of Mr. Bryant and demanded him to stop the meetings, and also forbid him to have prayers with his family; but like Daniel of old, he purposed in his heart to obey God rather than man, and the meetings were continued, amid threats, showers of stones and rains of lead.

During these years of revivals and persecutions, Mr. Spurling often came in their midst, and in vain tried to show the precious people the need of God's law and government. Everything moved on smoothly among themselves for several months, even years, and they were able to endure all the persecutions heaped upon them with grace and love. But in the absence of government and authority, false teachers crept in and led many humble, sincere, unwary souls into error. Factions began to show themselves, and fanaticism took possession of some who were more easily duped by Satan than others.

About that time Mr. Bryant and a few others began to see the mistake in being without government and authority, but as they were unable to accomplish anything on that line the work was allowed to drift. It is estimated that more than one hundred persons really received the baptism with the Holy Ghost and spoke in tongues as the evidence during that revival.

It was not until May 15, 1902, that any plan for government was adopted. On that day a number of humble people met at the home of Mr. Bryant, Cherokee county, N. C., and under the instructions and supervision of Mr. Spurling, an organization was effected. While this was a continuation of the same organization that was started sixteen years before, yet it was not given the same name, as it was in a different locality. It was called "The Holiness Church at Camp Creek," in Cherokee county, N. C. One of the officers, W. F. Bryant, was set forth by the church and ordained, which made the church permanent.

R. G. Spurling was chosen pastor, and they continued their meetings; yet the work was rather slow to develop, as so many had been led into error by the false teaching referred to above, but a sufficient number remained true to keep the work alive. For a year it was a real struggle to hold the organization against much unbelief and criticism, and there were no additions.

It was in June, 1903, that the work revived and took upon it a new impetus. At a meeting held June 13, of the above named year, we made a more careful study of the New Testament order, and five more accepted the obligation and joined with the faithful little flock to push the work along. Another minister and two deacons were ordained by the church in proper order. The new minister was chosen for pastor, and that year there were fourteen more accessions, and the work went on smoothly and prospered amid some light persecutions. One among the number added that year was M. S. Lemons.

The next year one organization was effected in Georgia and two more in Tennessee. Then the workers had increased, and evangelism was encouraged, so the work grew and prospered under the blessings and approval of God.

Near the close of 1905 the work had so prospered that there began to be a demand for a general gathering together of members from all the churches to consider questions of importance and to search the Bible for additional light and knowledge. Accordingly arrangements were made and the meeting called.

The first Assembly of the Churches of God was held January 26 and 27, 1906, at the home of J. C. Murphy, Cherokee county, N. C., about one-half mile from the school house where the great revival had broken out ten years before. Twenty-one members were in attendance as representatives from the different churches. Many important questions were discussed, and much added light obtained by those present.

The Second Annual Assembly was held at Union Grove, a meeting house in the country, ten miles from Cleveland, Tenn. Up to this time there had been but little said about the name of the church, except "The Church of God" had gradually come into use in conversation and preaching. But by this time we were getting thoroughly awakened on Scriptural themes and Apostolic teachings and practices regarding the church. Subjects and questions were discussed freely, with a view to coming fully to the Bible standard and plan for the Bible Church.

At a session held at 8:30 on Friday morning, January 11, 1907, the name "Church of God" was adopted, with the addition of the name of the place or locality where it existed. Examples: "The Church of God" at Cleveland, Tenn.; "The Church of God" at London, Ky., etc. This, however, was not meant to debar the use of the other Scriptural names, such as: "The Church," "Churches in Christ," "Church

* * * * in God our Father and the Lord Jesus Christ," etc.

The Third Annual Assembly was held January 8-12, 1908, at Cleveland, Tenn., and they have been held at the same place each successive year since. Every year has been more and more prosperous. The number of churches and membership have increased until at the Eighth Annual Assembly, held January 7-12, 1913, there was reported 104 churches in TEN different States, and the Bahama Islslands, with a total membership of 3,056. The report also shows forty-six Bishops, one hundred and twelve Deacons and sixty-one Evangelists.

The obligation has gradually assumed a broader and more elaborate form, because of a demand for it, and the need for a fuller explanation, so as to protect the church against some who might not be sincere and thoroughly conscientious. Following is nearly the common form of explanation and obligation:

As Jesus Christ is the sole founder and originator of His Church, and still retains the position as head and only lawgiver, all who connect themselves with His Church will be expected to obey His laws and government, walking in the light as He is in the light, thus giving fellowship to each other and the assurance of the blood cleansing from all sin. (1 John 1:7.)

The applicants for membership are expected to accept the teaching of repentance, water baptism (by immersion), sanctification subsequent to conversion, the baptism with the Holy Ghost on the sanctified life evidenced by the speaking in tongues as the Spirit gives utterance, the Lord's Supper, feet washing, eternal punishment for the wicked and eternal life for the righteous, divine healing, tithing and offerings, and the second pre-millenial coming of the Lord. Applicants must sever their connection with churches and lodges, if not already free from them.

Men having two or more wives, divorced or undivorced, and women having two or more husbands, divorced or undivorced, should not publicly present themselves for membership, but if they wish to join the church they should apply to the pastor or church privately, and be examined as to reasons for being so situated. Those using tobacco in any form should not present themselves for membership.

The obligation is simple, and just what every true child of God desires to practice.

Will you sincerely promise before God and these witnesses that you will take the Bible as your guide, the New Testament as your rule of faith and practice, government and discipline, and walk in the light to the best of your knowledge and ability?

Having accepted the above explanation and obligation the applicants are usually asked to kneel in holy reverence before God, while the minister engages in prayer and asks God's guidance and blessings upon the new members, and to make them useful, and keep them true and faithful until Jesus comes or calls.

When the prayer is ended a song is usually sung by the congregation, and all the members give them a glad welcome by extending to them the right hands of fellowship.

The Church recognizes three orders of ministers at present, but two more orders were mentioned in the Seventh Annual Assembly. The three now recognized are first, Bishops, second, Deacons, and third, Evangelists.

Applicants for the ministry are carefully and prayerfully examined as to their qalifications. It is expected that every examination conform strictly to the New Testament, and that all applicants measure to the requirements given therein before ordination. Paul's instructions to Timothy and Titus are strictly observed. It is against the rules of the Church to ordain or license any one who is a member of any lodge or society outside of the Church of God. The use of tobacco is forbidden, and under no circumstances can one be placed in the ministry who is addicted to its use.

There is also a strictness on the part of the Church

about men or women having two or more living wives or husbands, divorced or undivorced. Under no circumstances is it allowable to place one in the ministry who has more than one living wife, divorced or undivorced, if he pretends to live with either one; and no one can be ordained Bishop or Deacon who has a wife and does not live with her for any cause.

"Christ also loved the church, and gave himself for it; that he might sanctify and cleanse it with the washing of water by the word, that he might present it to himself a glorious church, not having spot, or wrinkle, or any such thing; but that it should be holy and without blemish." (Eph. 5:25-27.)

"Arise, shine; for thy light is come, and the glory of the Lord is risen upon thee. For, behold, the darkness shall cover the earth, and gross darkness the people: but the Lord shall arise upon thee, and his glory shall be seen upon thee. And the Gentiles shall come to thy light, and kings to the brightness of thy rising. Lift up thine eyes round about, and see: all they gather themselves together, they come to thee" (Isa. 60:1-4.)

"Therefore the redeemed of the Lord shall return, and come with singing unto Zion; and everlasting joy shall be upon their head: they shall obtain gladness and joy; and sorrow and mourning shall flee away." (Isa. 51:11.)

"Thy watchmen shall lift up the voice; with the

voice together shall they sing: for they shall see eye to eye, when the Lord shall bring again Zion." (Isa. 52:8.)

"Enlarge the place of thy tent, and let them stretch forth the curtains of thy habitations; spare not, lengthen thy cords, and strengthen thy stakes; for thou shalt break forth on the right hand and on the left; and thy seed shall inherit the Gentiles, and make the desolate cities to be inhabited." (Isa. 54: 2, 3.)

"In righteousness shalt thou be established: * * * * whosoever shall gather together against thee shall fall for thy sake. * * * * No weapon that is formed against thee shall prosper, and every tongue that shall rise against thee in judgment thou shalt condemn. This is the heritage of the servants of the Lord, and their righteousness is of me, saith the Lord." (Isa. 54:14-17.)

CHAPTER XXI.

EXPERIENCE.

At the age of twelve I had some slight convictions about eternal things. A little incident was the means of awakening my then spiritual nature.

Reared in a moral rural district among **Quakers**, I knew but little at that age about sin, neither did I know anything about the Bible or religion. My parents very seldom attended religious worship, **and** of course I did not go. I went to school in winter and worked on the farm in the spring and summer.

One day while father and myself were alone in the field a mile from home, sawing a large log with an old fashioned "Hoosier" cross-cut saw, I heard my name called, and thought father spoke to me. It was my familiar, family, pet name, but father said he did not speak it. In a few minutes I heard the same voice and the same name. Again father said he did not say a word. I was in a state of wonder. After a stillness of several minutes the voice spoke again, with that familiarity that is only recognized by the closest family ties. Father still said he did not call me nor speak my name. I was mystified, and although I never spoke to a soul about it, **and** father never said anything about it, it was enough to awaken a nature that had never been touched before, and it was awakened to never sleep again.

At the age of seventeen I graduated in my school and commenced to attend a high school in town. While there, quite a revival broke out in a church near the school house, and nearly all my schoolmates professed religion. My conscience and spiritual nature was thoroughly aroused, and many of my companions pleaded with me, besides others, but I would not yield.

It was after this that I caused my mother much anxiety and sleepless nights because she feared her boy was going to the bad.

I soon became much enthused about the political issues of the day, and was encouraged in it by my friends. I entered the campaign long before I was old enough to cast a ballot, and by my voice and influence put forth every effort I could, both day and night, for "my party."

During one campaign I became so enthusiastic and determined that I made a vow that if "my party" was defeated I was going to quit the United States and go to Australia. If "my party" was successful I would marry and settle down. The contest was severe, and I came near losing my life on account of my reckless enthusiasm, but we won the victory, and I married her that still abides with me, in my twenty-fourth year.

During all these years my conscience was lashing

me, except when in the most intense excitement. Even while on the stage, when the play was over late at night, I would retire, but could not sleep. Not a few times would I get up and kneel down and pray, and beg God for mercy, yet I knew nothing of salvation nor the Bible.

The first year of my married life I was one day engaged in hauling hay from one of those large Indiana meadows. A storm came up, and the men and myself hurried into the barn with what hay we had on the wagons. I ran on to the house so Mary would not be by herself during the storm. It was a very severe storm, with much lightning and heavy thunder. Suddenly a heavier peal of thunder than usual sounded so as to almost deafen us. Wife suggested that the lightning had struck the barn, but I said, "No, dear, it's the house." I saw the flash of lightning as it crashed down the chimney, out through the cook stove, and bursted out through the ceiling and weather boarding of the house only a few feet from where I was sitting. No serious damage was done, but it had an effect on me.

That evening after supper I said to wife, "It's time for us to pray," so I got the little Bible some one had given her (up to that time I did not care anything about the Bible), and read a few verses, and down we went to prayer. No doubt I was very awkward, but I was sincere. I meant everything I said. Wife had been a Christian for some time, and could pray, but it was my first experience in that way. Nothing much was accomplished that night, but I never let up until I got a real experience of salvation. My cards were soon cremated, and I was soon attending Sunday school.

Then came a real conflict: What church should I join? If there had been but one, as was the case in the time of the Apostles, I would have been saved that trouble. I searched and prayed and sought for information from people, books and papers. I was perplexed. I felt I was at a crisis. I did not know what to do. They were all different, and none of them really satisfied me, but I felt I must be a member of some church. If I had only known the Bible Church then! I finally decided to join the one nearest to my home, merely for convenience, as I thought I could do more good in one near by, as I could attend more regularly.

They soon put me in Superintendent of the Sunday school, and the little school of thirty soon ran up to sixty. Then a revival broke down upon us out of our prayer meeting. I could not preach, but somebody had to do something, and the older members and ministers were not inclined to take it off my hands except on Sunday, so I would go and get up before the congregation, and sometimes lose my text and could not find it, but I'd read whatever my eye caught, and talk a little, and after a few, stammering, broken utterances, the people would fall into the altar and get converted. The influence spread so that some were converted at home who had not been to the meeting. Up to that time I had not studied my Bible.

Some little time later I fell into a tremendous conflict with an "old man" who gave me a violent contest. I fought him and wrestled with him day and night for several months. How to conquer him I did not know. Nobody could tell me or give me much encouragement. I had some serious thoughts of building a little booth out in the middle of a certain field, where I could be alone with God and the Bible. Nobody could help me, so I did not want to be where they were. I was making a corn crop, and I suppose I prayed in nearly every row, and nearly all over the field. Though I worked hard every day, I frequently ate but one meal a day. I remember it as if it were but yesterday. I would leave the house at night at times, and stay out and pray for hours. I searched my Bible and prayed many nights till midnight and two o'clock, and then out at work again next morning by sun up. It was a hard fight, but I was determined for that "old man" to die. He had already given me much trouble, and I knew he would continue to do so if he was not slain. I saw it, and I knew he must be destroyed or I would be ruined, and my soul dragged down to hell by his subtile influence and cruel grasp.

At last the final struggle came. It was a hand to hand fight, and the demons of hell seemed to be mustering their forces, and their ghastly forms and furious yells would no doubt have been too much for me had not the Lord of heaven sent a host of angels to assist me in that terrible hour of peril. But it was the last great conflict, and I managed, by some peculiar dexterity, to put the sword into him up to the hilt.

It was about twelve o'clock in the day. I cried out in the bitterness of my soul: "Now! Now! You've got to give it up now! Now!" I felt him begin to weaken and quiver. I kept the "Sword" right in him, and never let go. That sharp two-edged "Sword" was doing its deadly work. I did not pity him. I showed him no quarters. There we were in that attitude when all of a sudden came from above, like a thunderbolt from the skies, a sensational power that ended the conflict, and there lay the "old man" dead at my feet, and I was free from his grasp. Thank God! I could get a good free breath once more. It was an awful struggle, but the victory was won. That was about twenty years ago, but it is fresh in my memory yet. I was indeed sanctified wholly.

Soon after this experience, a cry arose in my

heart for the same experience that was enjoyed by the people on the day of Pentecost. I called meetings to tarry and seek for the Pentecostal experience. But few were interested, and nothing much was accomplished. I was accused of being fanatical, but I cared nothing for that. I was hungry for God, and did not care who knew it.

During that time a little incident occurred that greatly strengthened my faith in regard to temporal supplies. I owed a debt of one hundred dollars. The note came due, and I was informed by the holder that he would have to have his money by a certain day. I had nothing, and nobody cared to help me. I did not know what to do. The day before I had to have the money I worked hard all day. In the evening I came in and sat down to eat my scanty meal. The blessing was asked on the food, and when I was about to eat, a queer feeling began to creep over me. I waited a moment to see what it meant, when suddenly I fell off my chair weeping, screaming and struggling. This lasted for several minutes. The suffering and agonizing was intense. The experience was a new one, but I realized it was a struggle with satan to loose his grasp on one hundred dollars so God could move some one to help me out in this time of extraordinary extremity. As I came to myself I fully realized that the victory was won, but I did not know how it would come about.

Suffice it to say that the money came from a very unexpected source, but God made me able to pay off the note the next day, at the very time it had been demanded. I have been trusting God for support ever since that time.

It would be too much, and probably useless, to tell about the experiences of traveling with no money sometimes since that time. Of going to the station without a cent, and hearing the whistle blow for the station, and yet no money and no ticket, and how, as the train rolled up, on I would go with the other passengers with my ticket in my hand, or starting to go hundreds of miles, sometimes a thousand, with only a few cents, or maybe half a dollar, and getting through safe and no delays; and giving the ticket agent all I had and get a ticket as far as that would buy it, and by the time I would get to that place my way would be paid still farther, and so on I would go.

It might not be necessary either to tell how my faithful companion and children have gone to bed hungry more than once, and sometimes lived on potatoes and salt for days, and their clothes so scant that they were hardly fit to go to meeting, while I was away from home in the Master's service, and never a murmur nor complaint.

I will here only give a hint of a mob being formed against me, and I felt like I was hunted down like a wild beast. And while I was absent another mob came to my home thinking I was there, and showered the rocks and clubs in through the windows on my wife and then little children, and only through God's peculiar providence was my son, Homer, saved alive. And at another time the bullets showered around us like hail as they poured volley after volley into our room, seemingly with the intention of sweeping us off the face of the earth.

Only a short time after these mobs had engaged themselves in these persecutions, one after another met with serious accidents and injuries, until it was the general talk, and fear came upon many who had spoken and taken a stand against the Holiness people. One shot himself accidentally, another fell into a furnace of melted ore at a smelting furnace, another was taken with fever and died, another, a Baptist preacher, got his house burned and destroyed everything he had, another sinned against God, according to his own testimony, until he declared he was doomed for hell.

There is a land of pure delight,
     Where trials and troubles ne'er shall come,
Be faithful here while in the light,
     And then you'll hear His sweet "well done "

As years roll by and toils increase,

And satan's howls are heard,
Think of the joy that ne'er shall cease,
Where foes no more disturb.

CHAPTER XXII.

EXPERIENCE—CONTINUED.
RECEVING THE HOLY GHOST

I knew I was converted. God gave me the witness of the fact by His Spirit, and many evidences in my life proved unmistakably that I was a child of God.

I knew I was sanctified. The experience was too real to entertain doubts about it. My very nature was changed. My soul craved nothing but God. The world began to fade from view; and lose its charms, as far as having a desire for its pleasures and possessions was concerned.

My interest in politics vanished so rapidly that I was almost surprised at myself when campaign year came around and found nothing in me craving the excitements of conventions, rallies and public speakings. I was so taken up with Jesus, and so bent on electing Him, that one day as I was walking along the road a gentleman met me and shouted out just like I had usually done, "Hurrah for M——!" With hardly a thought, and no premeditation, and yet with real enthusiasm, I shouted back at Him, "Hurrah for Jesus!" He was so startled and amazed that as he rode on and looked back at me he looked as if he wondered if I had just escaped from the lunatic asylum.   But he said no more, and went on.

My friends and neighbors begged me to at least go to the polls and vote, but I said, "No, I will only vote for Jesus." Their kindness, their friendship, their entreaties and reasoning had no more effect on me than if I had been in another world. I was dead to the world and the world was dead to me. I never have taken any part in politics since, nor gone to the polls and cast a ballot. When I was sanctified my whole nature was changed, and my whole being was almost constantly going out after God. I was almost incessantly seeking for the full baptism with the Holy Ghost.

In January, 1907, I became more fully awakened on the subject of receiving the Holy Ghost as He was poured out on the day of Pentecost. That whole year I ceased not to preach that it was our privilege to receive the Holy Ghost and speak in tongues as they did on the day of Pentecost. I did not have the experience, so I was almost always among the seekers at the altar. The Lord gave great revivals, and souls were converted and sanctified, and some really went through and were baptized with the Holy Ghost. evidenced by the speaking in tongues.

, By the close of the year I was so hungry for the Holy Ghost that I scarcely cared for food, friendship or anything else.   I wanted the one thing—the Bap-

tism with the Holy Ghost. I wrote to **G. B. Cash-**
well, who had been to Los Angeles, Cal., **and re-**
ceived the baptism there, and asked him to come to
our place for a few days. He arrived January 10,
1908. He preached on Saturday night, and on Sunday morning, January 12, while he was preaching, **a**
peculiar sensation took hold of me, and almost unconsciously I slipped off my chair in a heap on the
rostrum at Brother Cashwell's feet. I did not know
what such an experience meant. My mind was
clear, but a peculiar power so enveloped and thrilled
my whole being that I concluded to yield myself up
to God and await results   I was soon lost to my
surroundings as I lay there on the floor, occupiĕd
only with God and eternal things. Soon one of my
feet began to shake and clatter against the wall. I
could not hold it still. When it got quiet the other
one acted the same way. Then my arms and head
were operated. My jaws seemed to be set, my lips
were moved and twisted about as if a physician
was making a special examination. My tongue and
eyes were operated on in like manner. Several ex-
aminations seemed to be taken, and every limb and
my whole body examined.

My body was rolled and tossed about beyond
my control, and finally while lying on my back, my
feet were raised up several times, and my tongue
would stick out of my mouth in spite of my efforts

to keep it inside my mouth.

At one time, while lying flat on my back, I seemed to see a great sheet let down, and as it came to me I felt it as it enveloped me in its folds, and I really felt myself literally lifted up and off the floor several inches, and carried in that sheet several feet in the direction my feet pointed, and then let down on the floor again.   As I lay there great joy flooded my soul.   The happiest moments I had ever known up to that time.   I never knew what real joy was before.   My hands clasped together with no effort on my part.   Oh, such floods and billows of glory ran through my whole being for several minutes!   There were times that I suffered the most excruciating pain and agony, but my spirit always said "yes" to God.

Then came a very interesting part of the experience.   "They shall see visions."   In vision I was carried to Central America, and was shown the awful condition of the people there.   A paroxysm of suffering came over me as I seemed to be in soul travail for their salvation.   Then I spoke in tongues as the Spirit gave utterance, and in the vision I seemed to be speaking the very same language of the Indian tribes with whom I was surrounded.

Then after a little rest I was carried in vision to South America, and of all the black pictures that was ever painted that was surely the blackest.   The vision settled on Brazil, and after another paroxysm of suffering or soul travail the Spirit spoke again in another tongue; then after a little relaxation I was carried to Chili, with the same effects and results; then in like manner to Patagonia, away down among those illiterate Indians. Each place I was shown I gave assent in my spirit to go to them.

From Patagonia to Africa, and on to Jerusalem, and while there I endured the most intense suffering, as if I might have been suffering similar to that of my Savior on Mount Calvary. I never can describe the awful agony that I felt in my body. After every paroxysm of suffering came a tongue. From Jerusalem I was carried to Northern Russia, then to France, thence to Japan, and then I seemed to get back to the United States, but soon I was taken away North among the Espuimeaux. While there the language of the Spirit spoken through me seemed similar to the bark of a dog. I was carried to a number of other places in a similar manner.

I must not fail to tell of the terrible conflict I had in the vision with the devil. I came in direct contact with him. While in this state came the most awful struggle of all. While talking in an unknown tongue the Spirit seemed to envelope me, and I was taken through a course of casting out devils. A real experience in the vision, and the last verses of

Mark sixteen came very vividly before my mind.

In the vision I could see multitudes of people awakened and coming this way. Among them were Mrs. Tomlinson and my children. (They all received the baptism a few months later.) I saw us all on a missionary journey. Glory to God! This was really being baptized with the Holy Ghost as they received Him on the day of Pentecost.

With all I have written it is not yet told, but judging from the countries I visited in the vision I spoke ten different languages. It seemed that the Spirit was showing me these countries with a view to sending me there. Each place I saw large numbers of people coming to the light. I saw multitudes coming to Jesus. I do not know whether God wants me to go to these places or not, but I am certainly willing to go as He leads.

Since having received this wonderful experience —being baptized with the Holy Ghost as they were baptized on the day of Pentecost—God has revealed Himself and given many special manifestations of His presence and power in my life. Three times since, the same power has enveloped me and lifted me up from the floor similar to the way He lifted me up the day He came in to abide. Three times during special manifestations of His presence, truthful witnesses have seen "like as of fire" resting near and around my head.

I have traveled thousands of miles and told the simple story, and related my experience to thousands of people, and have seen hundreds baptized with the Holy Ghost, and every one who received Him spake in tongues as the Spirit gave them utterance.

I have seen whole congregations rise to their feet instantly as God's power ran with a thrill in all parts of the congregation. At other times I've seen nearly whole audiences on their faces before God as that same thrill of power ran like lightning in every direction. At one time as I stepped out to make an altar call, as I lifted my hands, a kind of blue mist was seen by a number of truthful witnesses as it settled down on the congregation, and not a few fell, and either crawled or were carried into the altar. A few times while the words were spoken, the Holy Ghost fell on all that heard the Word. Streaks of fire have been seen as they darted just above the heads of the people in the congregation, like zigzag lightning, and yet not so quick but that it was easily seen by scores of people.

On the night of January 3, 1909, while God's power was being so wonderfully demonstrated on the inside of the house, a large ball of fire was seen to pass just in front of the door of the church house. A sign of a peculiar character was seen in the heavens about the same time. The same night, or at

another time at the same place, there was seen a
ball of fire descend from above, and as it struck the
roof of the house, just above the pulpit and altar,
where so much of God's presence was being demonstrated, it broke into fragments and rolled and
sparkled over the roof.

On Tuesday morning just before day, November
23, 1909, a peculiar phenomenon was witnessed by
two of our neighbors. Just above our house appeared a light, similar in appearance to a head-light
of a locomotive. It was in motion, moving up and
down. It would be hidden from their view a few
moments, then make its appearance again. This
lasted for several seconds, probably minutes, then
vanished from their sight. That day was one of
weeping and agonizing prayer in my room with a
few of the brethren. We knew nothing of the light
above the house for several days afterward.

A little note from my journal would probably not
be out of order here: "May 27. Yesterday was a
wonderful day in the camp. In the beginning of the
service in the morning, one or two messages were
given in tongues, and I gave the interpretation. Afterward I was seized with two or three spells of
weeping, and finally fell on my back under the
overwhelming power of God. After screaming for
a while as though my heart would break, I became
a little more quiet, when a brother spoke a few

words in tongues and they said I gave the interpretation, which was, "Get quiet and hear me speak." Immediately a sister began to speak in tongues, and the interpretation followed: the tongues in a few words, and then the few words interpreted alternately, until the sentence was finished. I was told this lasted for half an hour. When she ceased, some one else spoke a few minutes and the interpretations followed; then another and another and another. Some one said I was prostrated there for two hours. That was all the preaching that was done. The altar was full of seekers crying out to God when I arose. The meeting that followed during the day is indescribable. Men, women and children screaming, shouting, praying, leaping, dancing and falling prostrate under God's overwhelming power. Wonderful!"

June 24. "Meetings have been going on every day and night; sometimes continuing from six o'clock in the morning till nearly midnight without a break. Many signs and wonders have been done by myself, my son Homer and others by the power of the Spirit.

A brother had been seeking long, but had failed to get through. I was led, in the Spirit, to go to him on my knees, stretch his arms out and nail his hands to the cross, then to fall over with him in my arms and go through the death struggle for him.

Then after I had been as though dead for a little while, I arose and appeared to pierce his side and cut off his head; then to put him in the grave and cover him up with earth. He lay there a while quiet, and then I made as though I removed the covering of earth, and he was resurrected, and at that moment the power struck him, and he soon received the baptism with the Holy Ghost.

It is wonderful what is taking place here. Yesterday afternoon, after I had been preaching a little while, the power fell, and I fell into agonizing cries, and when I opened my eyes the altar was crowded with seekers. More than once the altar calls have been made in tongues by some one, and I gave the interpretations. One night a sister stepped upon the altar rail by my side while I was preaching and gave a message in tongues and I gave the interpretations, and the people flocked into the altar to seek God. Fear is falling upon many. People are getting saved, sanctified and filled with the Holy Ghost.''

Many similar experiences could be given, but suffice it to say that the experience God gave me on the twelfth day of January, 1908, is still abiding, and still fresh and sweet this first day of February, 1913.

The experiences, blessings and victories God has given, have not been without severe trials, testings, oppositions and some slight persecutions, but in every instance God has stood by me and given grace, and brought me through more than conqueror. And I feel that these light afflictions will work out for me a far more exceeding and eternal weight of glory.

"For we know that if our earthly house of this tabernacle were dissolved, we have a building of God, an house not made with hands, eternal in the heavens."

I expect my life to count for God and humanity in this last great conflict, as we wage a warfare against sin and satan; false teaching, infidelity, higher criticism and the evolution theory.

Oh, for a million men who would fear nothing but God, filled with such holy zeal and Godly courage, that we could all together burst forth under the power of this mighty baptismal fire and rush to every quarter of the globe like mad men, declaring the gospel of the Son of God, until every tribe, kindred, tongue and people could hear, and thus end this Last Great Conflict!

THE END.

TITLES in THIS SERIES

geles, 1925), *AROUND THE WORLD BY FAITH, WITH SIX WEEKS IN THE HOLY LAND* (Los Angeles, n. d.), *TWO YEARS MISSION WORK IN EUROPE JUST BEFORE THE WORLD WAR, 1912-14* (Los Angeles, [1926])

6. Boardman, W. E., *THE HIGHER CHRISTIAN LIFE* (Boston, 1858)

7. Girvin, E. A., *PHINEAS F. BRESEE: A PRINCE IN ISRAEL* (Kansas City, Mo., [1916])

8. Brooks, John P., *THE DIVINE CHURCH* (Columbia, Mo., 1891)

9. RUSSELL KELSO CARTER ON "FAITH HEALING." R. Kelso Carter, *THE ATONEMENT FOR SIN AND SICKNESS* (Boston, 1884) *"FAITH HEALING" REVIEWED AFTER TWENTY YEARS* (Boston, 1897)

10. Daniels, W. H., *DR. CULLIS AND HIS WORK* (Boston, [1885])

11. HOLINESS TRACTS DEFENDING THE MINISTRY OF WOMEN. Luther Lee, *"WOMAN'S RIGHT TO PREACH THE GOSPEL; A SERMON, AT THE ORDINATION OF REV. MISS ANTOINETTE L. BROWN, AT SOUTH BUTLER, WAYNE COUNTY, N. Y., SEPT. 15, 1853"* (Syracuse, 1853) *bound with* B. T. Roberts, *ORDAINING WOMEN* (Rochester, 1891) *bound with* Catherine (Mumford) Booth, *"FEMALE MINISTRY; OR, WOMAN'S RIGHT TO PREACH THE GOSPEL . . ."* (London, n. d.) *bound with* Fannie (McDowell) Hunter, *WOMEN PREACHERS* (Dallas, 1905)

12. LATE NINETEENTH CENTURY REVIVALIST TEACHINGS ON THE HOLY SPIRIT. D. L. Moody, *SECRET POWER OR THE SECRET OF SUCCESS IN CHRISTIAN LIFE AND*

Work (New York, [1881]) *bound with* J. Wilbur Chapman, *Received Ye the Holy Ghost?* (New York, [1894]) *bound with* R. A. Torrey, *The Baptism with the Holy Spirit* (New York, 1895 & 1897)

13. Seven "Jesus Only" Tracts. Andrew D. Urshan, *The Doctrine of the New Birth, or, the Perfect Way to Eternal Life* (Cochrane, Wis., 1921) *bound with* Andrew Urshan, *The Almighty God in the Lord Jesus Christ* (Los Angeles, 1919) *bound with* Frank J. Ewart, *The Revelation of Jesus Christ* (St. Louis, n. d.) *bound with* G. T. Haywood, *The Birth of the Spirit in the Days of the Apostles* (Indianapolis, n. d.) *Divine Names and Titles of Jehovah* (Indianapolis, n. d.) *The Finest of the Wheat* (Indianapolis, n. d.) *The Victim of the Flaming Sword* (Indianapolis, n. d.)

14. Three Early Pentecostal Tracts. D. Wesley Myland, *The Latter Rain Covenant and Pentecostal Power* (Chicago, 1910) *bound with* G. F. Taylor, *The Spirit and the Bride* (n. p., [1907?]) *bound with* B. F. Laurence, *The Apostolic Faith Restored* (St. Louis, 1916)

15. Fairchild, James H., *Oberlin: The Colony and the College, 1833-1883* (Oberlin, 1883)

16. Figgis, John B., *Keswick from Within* (London, [1914])

17. Finney, Charles G., *Lectures to Professing Christians* (New York, 1837)

18. Fleisch, Paul, *Die Moderne Gemeinschafts-bewegung in Deutschland* (Leipzig, 1912)

19. SIX TRACTS BY W. B. GODBEY. *SPIRITUAL GIFTS AND GRACES* (Cincinnati, [1895]) *THE RETURN OF JESUS* (Cincinnati, [1899?]) *WORK OF THE HOLY SPIRIT* (Louisville, [1902]) *CHURCH—BRIDE—KINGDOM* (Cincinnati, [1905]) *DIVINE HEALING* (Greensboro, [1909]) *TONGUE MOVEMENT, SATANIC* (Zarephath, N. J., 1918)

20. Gordon, Earnest B., *ADONIRAM JUDSON GORDON* (New York, [1896])

21. Hills, A. M., *HOLINESS AND POWER FOR THE CHURCH AND THE MINISTRY* (Cincinnati, [1897])

22. Horner, Ralph C., *FROM THE ALTAR TO THE UPPER ROOM* (Toronto, [1891])

23. McDonald, William and John E. Searles, *THE LIFE OF REV. JOHN S. INSKIP* (Boston, [1885])

24. LaBerge, Agnes N. O., *WHAT GOD HATH WROUGHT* (Chicago, n. d.)

25. Lee, Luther, *AUTOBIOGRAPHY OF THE REV. LUTHER LEE* (New York, 1882)

26. McLean, A. and J. W. Easton, *PENUEL; OR, FACE TO FACE WITH GOD* (New York, 1869)

27. McPherson, Aimee Semple, *THIS IS THAT: PERSONAL EXPERIENCES SERMONS AND WRITINGS* (Los Angeles, [1919])

28. Mahan, Asa, *OUT OF DARKNESS INTO LIGHT* (London, 1877)

29. THE LIFE AND TEACHING OF CARRIE JUDD MONTGOMERY Carrie Judd Montgomery, *"UNDER HIS WINGS": THE STORY OF MY LIFE* (Oakland,

[1936]) Carrie F. Judd, *THE PRAYER OF FAITH* (New York, 1880)

30. THE DEVOTIONAL WRITINGS OF PHOEBE PALMER Phoebe Palmer, *THE WAY OF HOLINESS* (52nd ed., New York, 1867) *FAITH AND ITS EFFECTS* (27th ed., New York, n. d., orig. pub. 1854)

31. Wheatley, Richard, *THE LIFE AND LETTERS OF MRS. PHOEBE PALMER* (New York, 1881)

32. Palmer, Phoebe, ed., *PIONEER EXPERIENCES* (New York, 1868)

33. Palmer, Phoebe, *THE PROMISE OF THE FATHER* (Boston, 1859)

34. Pardington, G. P., *TWENTY-FIVE WONDERFUL YEARS, 1889-1914: A POPULAR SKETCH OF THE CHRISTIAN AND MISSIONARY ALLIANCE* (New York, [1914])

35. Parham, Sarah E., *THE LIFE OF CHARLES F. PARHAM, FOUNDER OF THE APOSTOLIC FAITH MOVEMENT* (Joplin, [1930])

36. THE SERMONS OF CHARLES F. PARHAM. Charles F. Parham, *A VOICE CRYING IN THE WILDERNESS* (4th ed., Baxter Springs, Kan., 1944, orig. pub. 1902) *THE EVERLASTING GOSPEL* (n.p., n.d., orig. pub. 1911)

37. Pierson, Arthur Tappan, *FORWARD MOVEMENTS OF THE LAST HALF CENTURY* (New York, 1905)

38. *PROCEEDINGS OF HOLINESS CONFERENCES, HELD AT CINCINNATI, NOVEMBER 26TH, 1877, AND AT NEW YORK, DECEMBER 17TH, 1877* (Philadelphia, 1878)

39. *RECORD OF THE CONVENTION FOR THE PROMOTION OF*

SCRIPTURAL HOLINESS HELD AT BRIGHTON, MAY 29TH, TO JUNE 7TH, 1875 (Brighton, [1896?])

40. Rees, Seth Cook, MIRACLES IN THE SLUMS (Chicago, [1905?])

41. Roberts, B. T., WHY ANOTHER SECT (Rochester, 1879)

42. Shaw, S. B., ed., ECHOES OF THE GENERAL HOLINESS ASSEMBLY (Chicago, [1901])

43. THE DEVOTIONAL WRITINGS OF ROBERT PEARSALL SMITH AND HANNAH WHITALL SMITH. [R]obert [P]earsall [S]mith, HOLINESS THROUGH FAITH: LIGHT ON THE WAY OF HOLINESS (New York, [1870]) [H]annah [W]hitall [S]mith, THE CHRISTIAN'S SECRET OF A HAPPY LIFE, (Boston and Chicago, [1885])

44. [S]mith, [H]annah [W]hitall, THE UNSELFISHNESS OF GOD AND HOW I DISCOVERED IT (New York, [1903])

45. Steele, Daniel, A SUBSTITUTE FOR HOLINESS; OR, ANTINOMIANISM REVIVED (Chicago and Boston, [1899])

46. Tomlinson, A. J., THE LAST GREAT CONFLICT (Cleveland, 1913)

47. Upham, Thomas C., THE LIFE OF FAITH (Boston, 1845)

48. Washburn, Josephine M., HISTORY AND REMINISCENCES OF THE HOLINESS CHURCH WORK IN SOUTHERN CALIFORNIA AND ARIZONA (South Pasadena, [1912?])